Iceberg Sighted: Decision-Making
Techniques to avoid titanic disasters

Miguel Angel Ariño
Pablo Maella

newcelona.com

Iceberg Sighted: Decision-Making
Techniques to avoid titanic disasters

Miguel Angel Ariño y Pablo Maella

Translated from the original in spanish
"*Iceberg a la vista, 10 principios para la toma de decisiones*"

Versión P.O.D. - 1a Edición - Enero 2013

ISBN: 978-84-935593-2-8

TABLE OF CONTENTS

INTRODUCTION

TEN FUNDAMENTAL PRINCIPLES FOR DECIDING EFFECTIVELY

CONCLUSION   93

INTRODUCTION

Just in case anyone still does not know the story, the *Titanic* was an enormous, luxurious passenger ship that sank when it crashed into an iceberg on the night of the fourteenth and the morning of the fifteenth of April of 1912, during her inaugural voyage from England to the United States. The collision provoked one of the biggest disasters that the history of navigation has ever known, causing more than 1,500 deaths.

The most advanced techniques available at the time were used in the ship's construction, hence it was popularly known by the name: "the unsinkable". The dimensions of the boat were the largest of its era: a length of 269 meters, a width of 28 meters and a height of 56 meters. It could transport some three thousand five hundred and fifty people, although in its first and last voyage it carried about two thousand, two hundred and thirty, including the eight hundred and ninety-seven people who made up the crew. Only some seven hundred individuals survived the accident.

Many studies of this fact have affirmed that it was an inevitable accident, due to the fact that a sequence of events led unfailingly to the ship's sinking. However, other analysts maintain that the disaster could have been avoided if different decisions had been made. In the following chapters, we will use the example of the *Titanic* to illustrate the process of making decisions and their possible consequences and analyze some of the decisions that were made before, during, and after the disaster.

The Importance of Making Decisions

We learn to walk by walking. We learn to swim by swimming. But, we don't learn to make decisions only by making decisions. One learns to decide when one internalizes certain basic principles, which we will attempt to transmit over the course of this book. Some of these principles could seem very basic and elementary, but they are exactly the obvious things that we often don´t take into account and lead us to ineffective decisions. Our lives and also the organizations of which we form a part, depend on two factors: the decisions we make and the external environment. The external environment is comprised of all of those circumstances that surround us and over which we have no control and no manner of influencing. The smart person or the dumb person, the tallest or the shortest, the French, American or Ethiopian; to have been born in the second half of the twentieth century or in the sixteenth century are circumstances that affect us, but about which we can do nothing. We must live with these circumstances whether we like them or not. Since we can do nothing, the best thing to do is to accept these circumstances as points of departure for our lives. The desire to be something that we are not and that is not part of our way of being only will be a point of frustration. It is best to accept the reality in which we live and not to long for what could have been. By accepting the external environment and being conscious that we will not always be capable of resolving all of the problems that we face, we can make more realistic decisions.

Something distinct happens when these other circumstances accompany us in life and over which we have the possibility of influencing. Over some, we will have total control and over others, we will simply be able to have influence to a certain degree. We control or influence all of these circumstances by the decisions we make. It is for this reason that in the future, what our lives are like, depends on the decisions we make over the course of time, because by making these decisions is how we influence our reality. We can say that our personal history is the history of the decisions we have made, and our future – which is conditioned by those decisions we have already made – we will shape through our future decisions. From here, we see the importance of making decisions in the lives of people; at the end of the day, each one of us is what we decide to be. In the ambit of management, it is the fundamental act of a director, since a director is the person who is deciding.
Making decisions is so closely aligned to our lives that we can not disregard it: we cannot abstain from making decisions because to decide

not to make a decision implicates us as much as having made one. What we can decide is whether we would like to make our decisions or prefer that others make them for us. In this case, we are deciding to give control of our lives to third parties. For this reason, we cannot renounce deciding because by doing so we convert ourselves into spectators instead of into actors in our existence.

We cannot subcontract making decisions, as opposed to, for example, the management of the assets of the company. Each person is irremediably obligated, by action or by omission, to make decisions. For these reasons, it is good to accustom oneself to making decisions actively, even if they are about little things. This is a habit that is strengthened with practice and without which one becomes paralyzed. If we accustom ourselves to not making decisions proactively, it will make it more difficult to make them, because indecision generates more indecision.

With every decision there is always the possibility of error. There are people who tend to not make decisions because they fear making a mistake and they let circumstances decide for them, thereby abandoning control of their own existence. These types of people, who refuse the possibility of failing, paradoxically end up doing so because by not deciding they have no possibilities to emerge from the situation to find success. By renouncing the possibility of failing, you renounce the possibility of success as well.

Successful people have also had misfortunes. People considered great businesspeople accumulate failures in their lives, some of them sensational. Success is often the result of failure. Being successful is made up of getting up one more time than the times you have fallen. If we don´t try, we cannot win. If I don´t buy a ticket, I won´t win the lottery.

Principles Exist to Decide Well

People make decisions to solve problems that are presented and they do this in the form that they think best. But, many times we become distracted as to whether the choice made is the best one or not for resolving the problem that we have.

What can we do? Well, we can follow a series of principles that exist to assure a correct process for making decisions. These principles will not tell us what alternative we have to choose in each moment nor how to solve the problem that we have, but they will indicate characteristics of the alternatives we need to choose between so as not to make a mistake. They are a type of checklist that we have to verify each time we make a decision. Whoever incorporates the habit of following these principles for making decisions, will end up doing this the best.

Fortunately, the majority of times we unconsciously apply these principles in an intuitive manner. They are the routine ways we have for approaching habitual situations. However, there are occasions in which the decision requires a larger reflection and we need to take into account these principles explicitly.

Taking these principles into account never guarantees that the best decision is made, but it will allow us to avoid entering into a spiral of systematic errors. The application of these principles will create in us a habit that will, in many cases, allow us to decide intuitively. We will have acquired the habit of decision-making. To decide well each time will become easier and we will be prepared to correct errors and learn from them.

On the contrary, when we don´t follow these basic principles of making decisions, we can only aspire to decide and wait to see what happens. In this way, we leave the solution of problems to chance. When things turn out well for us, we attribute this success, thinking erroneously that the fact that the result has been favorable is a test that we have decided well, discarding the role of luck in the action. On the other hand, when things turn out badly, we become perplexed and don´t know why this has happened. Making decisions following guidelines allows us to learn how to make better decisions each time.

In the following chapters, we will approach distinct principles that are helpful to follow in order to guarantee that we learn to decide better each time. We will illustrate these guidelines with examples of the decisions that were made in the sinking of the *Titanic*.

TEN FUNDAMENTAL PRINCIPLES
FOR DECIDING EFFECTIVELY

01.

Concern Yourself With Deciding Well Rather Than With Being Correct

The night of the sinking of the *Titanic*, Captain Smith, who was in charge of the ship, acted in response to the first signs that they were entering a dangerous zone. But, the reaction was more symbolic than effective: it took place after the ship received the third message of alert, requiring that they slightly change direction to the south. Yet he did nothing more about the danger that the icebergs they would encounter would cause the ships, despite the fact that those warnings continued arriving throughout the afternoon and night. If Smith reacted at all, according to the experts, his reaction was demonstrably insufficient. Lightly changing the trajectory towards the south did not allow him to avoid the blocks of ice. He made a decision to solve a problem, but it was clearly insufficient to avoid the undesired effect, in this case, collision.

An experienced man like Smith, already knew this was not an adequate decision, that it left the ship in a very vulnerable situation, at the mercy of the iceberg, but surely he had the secret and naïve hope that this would be enough.

He decided in an incorrect manner with the hope of being lucky. It is for this reason that although he could have avoided the collision, the decision would have been incorrect. He made a bad decision with the hope that luck would make everything OK.

The passengers of the *Titanic's* third class were the last ones to learn about the accident. No one formally communicated to them, and, like the great majority of passengers, they were sleeping in their cabins until the movement of the evacuation of the boats on the deck of the ship was very obvious and they didn't realize the gravity of the situation in which they had found themselves. Given that from the third class area there was no free access to the decks where the life-boats were located, and given that the crew had orders not to open the access doors to passengers from third class, these passengers were forced to violently break the barriers that separated them from first class in order to be able to access the lifeboats.

As the leadership decided to first evacuate those passengers of first and second class, those of third class had to take the initiative them-selves in order to find a way of saving themselves. The result was that those who were able to access the boats ended up saving their lives. *But although all of the passengers of third class could have been saved, which wasn't the case, the decision to restrict access to the deck was in and of itself an incorrect decision because it limited the possibilities of survival.*

* * *

Deciding well is not the same as being sure. At times, one decides well, but unpredictable circumstances make it such that things don't turn out well. One should decide well and not try to be certain. Often, in our classes, we conduct a test in order to explain this fact. We offer a group of people the possibility to participate in a game. The game consists of taking a ball out of a urn. If the ball is white, they will receive 100 euros and if the ball is black they have to pay one euro. Additionally, we inform them that there are ninety-nine white balls in the urn and one black ball (something that they can check). After-wards, we ask how many of them agreed to participate? Obviously, all of them accepted the proposal. One innocent hand takes out a ball and it is black. Have they decided well or badly? Evidently, all of them have decided well. If the ball comes out black and they lose one euro it is exclusively for bad luck and not because they have made a bad decision. In fact, all of them agree to play a second time.

We could say that decisions are either correct or incorrect with re-spect to how one has decided and that they can be favorable or unfa-vorable with respect to the results. All of these considerations bring us to four possible situations as the following chart shows:

16

DECISION

		+		−	

		DECISION +	**DECISION −**
OUTCOMES	**+**	OK	MINIMAL LEARNING
	−	BAD LUCK	POSSIBILITY TO LEARN

a) Correct Decision with Favorable Outcomes
In this situation everyone is happy and things work out well. Congratulations! There is nothing else to say. You have chosen the right path!

b) Correct Decision with Unfavorable Outcomes
Before the surprise of some unfavorable results, the most reasonable is to review the decision-making process. Perhaps these results were the consequence of an erroneous way of making decisions. After having revised the decision-making process we recognize that we may have decided well and simply gotten unfavorable results. In the long-term, everything is OK because if we decide correctly, although in a specific moment we are not sure, we end up with the results. In this case, it was simply bad luck. It does not matter.

It does not matter? Well, wait a minute! It depends on your boss. If your boss is competent, therefore, it does not matter. It is understood that you have decided well. But if your boss is incompetent, he or she

17

will be incapable of seeing that the unexpected outcomes are not a result of an adequate decision-making process. If you had to do it over again in the same circumstances, you would make the same decision. If this is the case, you may wish to change your job.

c) Incorrect Decision with Unfavorable Outcomes
Your company cannot survive many situations like this one. However, this is a fairly frequent situation. It allows you and your company to learn from your errors and to improve your decision-making process. You will learn to keep in mind factors that you should have considered and did not.

Incorrect Decision and Favorable Results
You have had good luck. This is the most dangerous situation. The favorable results make one believe that one has decided well and, therefore, the inadequate method of deciding is confirmed. Definitely, one learns to decide badly. The only cause of the good results has been luck. But, if the success of your company is a result of favorable luck, what are you bringing to the company? Luck is what is driving the company, not you, and this is the most dangerous situation because luck sometimes helps you and sometimes goes against you.

Luck (good or bad) is the combination of unpredictable and uncontrollable factors that intervene in a situation. Frequently, directors have made incorrect decisions, although they could have had luck and the results of this decision have been favorable, and they foolishly attributed this success to their capabilities as directors and kept faultily saying this time and time again. They rested on their laurels without listening to those who suggested more sensible ways of making decisions. Time plays against these directors. In the medium term, the negative consequences of these defective ways of making decisions will come to light. If they decide badly, although they have been correct in the short-term, they will end up with bad results.

An example of bad decision-making when the objective is to try to be certain is that of some people who invest in the stock market.

When they try to make the most profit they are continuously buying and selling shares. They buy those that they have bought only a few months earlier and sell those that they have only just recently purchased. The only people who benefit from this exhausting practice are the stockbrokers who make commissions on each transaction. And, as is logical, stockbrokers would like the maximum number of transactions to be made.

In contrast, the manner of operating of the richest man in the world, Warren Buffet, is completely the opposite. He invests is very few stocks, but he chooses them carefully and he commits himself for the long-term to the companies in which he chooses to invest. How does he do this? He first considers the principle that diversification diminishes risk as a certainty, but at the same time, a joke. It is certain that when you invest in a large number of stocks that go badly, you are left with those that go well, and, at the end, you are ensured a medium profit.

But, Warren Buffett says that what one must do is invest only in stocks of companies that are doing well and not in those that are not doing well. He only invests in a few companies that he considers good ones. He chooses companies where he understands the business, like Coca-Cola, whose business the entire world understands. For this same reason, he rejected the offer to invest in Enron, realizing that he did not understand this business. Additionally, Buffett also takes into consideration whether the company has a future, if it has a good strategy and if it has competent directors who are capable of successfully leading the business.

Once he has chosen a company with these characteristics, he evaluates it with a very simple methods and without much technical complexity. Afterwards, he takes into account the price of the stock in the market. If he finds it much beneath the value that he has calculated, he will invest in it, maintain his investment for the long-term and not worry about fluctuations in the stock price. On the one hand, because he has bought when the price was well below the value that he has calculated with his methods, he does not get preoccupied with the exactness of his methodology. On the other hand, as the company is solid and directed by competent individuals, in the long-term the price of his shares should go up and arrive at a level that corresponds with the value of the company.

This simple way of proceeding has allowed him to become, over time, the richest man in the world, richer even than Bill Gates. Meanwhile, other investors are buying and selling shares, trying to know when the price will go up and to avoid the next drop in price, all the time paying numerous small commissions that finally detract from the possible earnings. This is to say, that while trying to be right instead of deciding well, they end up being less efficient.

The fact that deciding well is not the same as being sure of the outcome, has various consequences. One of these is that the decisions of our colleagues should not be judged by the results. It could be that they have decided well and, however, the consequences of their decisions are not those that they intended.

If we do not allow our colleagues to make errors and if we penalize them for decisions that, although they may seem correct, do not yield satisfactory results, at decision-making time they will stop thinking about what is best for the the company as a whole and start thinking about what is best for themselves. Essentially, they will refrain from from taking on any reasonable and convenient risks for the company at all so as not to risk upsetting their superiors. As a result, it is advisable to leave people who are in our surroundings to make decisions although we cannot be sure of the outcomes.

A second consequence is that we cannot judge the decisions of a subordinate using information that is not available when we make the decision. In hindsight, people may know what they should have done; it is very easy to criticize things once they have already happened. But, the person who made the decision did so with many unresolved uncertainties and it is for this reason that in order to judge the quality of his decision one needs to put oneself in the situation the manager was in when he made the decision. That being said, you would be an incompetent boss if you were to judge the decisions of your subordinates based on future facts that came to be known after the decision was made. One cannot judge the quality of a decision using information that was not available at the time it was made. Not only is this unjust, it is also ineffective.

But the evaluation of decisions using information that was not available at the moment of making the decisions, is not only prejudicial when we evaluate the determinations of our collaborators, but it is also prejudicial when we analyze our own decisions, which can already be a self-destructive exercise. One can lament that one did not decide well, when one, in reality, made the best decision at the time taking into account the available information.

Making decisions to resolve matters that come up or that we provoke with the objective of bettering our situation, and only thinking that we have decided well when the matter has been resolved, and, in the opposite case, if nothing results we think we have decided badly, is a frequent error that we make when we make decisions.

Company XYZ, after a careful analysis of various alternatives, decided, at the end of 2000, to move their headquarters and the two hundred people who worked in their headquarters to floors 95 and 96 of one of the twin towers in New York. The move occurred during the summer of 2001 and normal activities started on Monday, September 10th. During the morning of the following day, the company's headquarters were destroyed and half of the staff perished.

Many people would say that, in light of the consequences, the decision to move the headquarters was an incorrect one. But, there is nothing further from the truth. In order to evaluate whether the result of the move was correct or not, it is important to consider if, through the analysis of distinct alternatives, enough attention was given to the pros and cons of each one. But, the fact that the day after the move there was a terrorist attack is something independent from the decision that was made various months earlier. It was not under

21

the control of the directors of this company to prevent the attack, which was not something that could have been taken into account when the decision was made.

It is important to understand this in making decisions, also to avoid frustration. To decide well will not always signify that you will reach the desired consequences. There will always be variables that we cannot foresee nor control and that will affect the results of our decisions. To believe that things will always work out the way we would like them to work out is equivalent to trying to control all of the variables that affect our world. As this is impossible, if we don´t take this into account beforehand, we will continually deceive ourselves.

We have to convince ourselves that we cannot control everything that is out of our reach. We must accept that many things are out of our control, and that, at times, bad things will happen to us for other reasons outside of our responsibility. We only can be responsible for things over which we have some margin of control. We are responsible for how we make decisions, not for the results in and of themselves.

A financial analyst who has a good reputation as a competent professional and who is honest with his clients, counsels one of them to invest his money in shares of a particular company. He explains that there is a twenty percent possibility that the stocks will be worth as much as the client hopes, but that, in spite of this, it appears that this is the best investment for the client since there is also a great potential for increase in value.

Over the period of a few months, the investment is not yielding high returns. Can it be said that the client made a bad decision in listening to the analyst? Not at all. The analyst warned him of the possibility of a bad return. If this is actually what happened, this was known from beforehand that this was a possibility and was presented as such, yet notwithstanding, the client accepted the risk.

This client would have made a bad decision if he would have accepted the advice of any random financial analyst without an established reputation, and without being sure that the analyst was truly competent. The decision would have been erroneous if the advice of a bad professional had been accepted when dealing with investments, regardless of the final result. The error would be independent on whether or not the company would have grown in value by 0% or by 100%.

Evading frustration is important since once frustrated, a person is likely to continue to make worse decisions. In the previous example, the client can lament and reprimand himself for having gone through with the investment. His frustration will probably lead him to make the decision to change analysts, a detrimental decision for him because he will no longer be able to count on the support of a competent professional.

Frustration lessens the efficacy of our decision-making ability, while fruitful learning from our decisions, whether correct or incorrect, with favorable or unfavorable results, favors the improvement of the efficacy in making decisions. If we learn from all the decisions taken, we can decide better every time.

SUMMARY OF IDEAS

• In the short-run, positive outcomes may be obtained with bad decisions and negative outcomes may be achieved deciding well. But, in the long-run, if you decide well, you will end up obtaining the intended results.

• You are responsible for how you make decisions, not of the results obtained from these decisions. Do not have an unjustified sense of responsibility.

• If you want to learn, analyze your decisions as a function of how you have made them and not only based on the results you achieve.

• Many times we make bad decisions, waiting— naïvely— And despite that we will will be correct, and we abandon ourselves to luck.

• *Do not base your assessment of past decisions on information that you have at your disposal in the present: it's self-destructive.*

02.

Clearly Identify Your Objectives

In the first years of the twentieth century, the ship was the most common means of transport for long distances. The companies operating in this sector centered their competitive efforts on being faster: the faster their ships were, the more prestige the company had. However, the British company, White Star, owner of the *Titanic,* modified its strategy and decided to compete for luxury and comfort rather than for speed.

As this was the objective, the ship needed to be large: a small boat would not have been constructed with ample staterooms, or spacious drawing rooms or recreation areas. That is to say, the very objective that White Star focused on later determined the decisions that were made to reach it. If the objective had been speed, the boat would have been made smaller in order to be faster. From here we can see the importance of establishing objectives while being conscious of what will be important later on. *It has to do with thinking carefully about the objectives you hope to reach, since whatever these objectives are will drive one to one type of decision or another.*

The chief executive of White Star, Bruce Ismay, publicly affirmed that the boat would complete the inaugural journey one day prior to that which was scheduled. Once he had made this promise, Ismay acted as a result of this decision, which implied that he needed to pressure Captain Smith not to reduce the sailing velocity in spite of the fact that there had been warnings about icebergs in the area in which they found themselves.

To arrive one day early is and would be a secondary goal at all times. Ismay´s emphasis on reaching secondary objectives implied that he would put the lives of hundreds of passengers in danger. Curiously, the company´s own director caused the sinking of the ship by not prioritizing his goals and by trying to achieve everything. If, by knowing that he would go through a field of icebergs, he would have renounced arriving one day before the day predicted, he could have slackened the gears and navigated between the ice floes with more care. *When we do not adequately prioritize and when we confuse secondary objectives with vital ones, we will necessarily make bad decisions.*

The diverse messages of alarm that were received the night of the sinking were not transmitted to the captain´s deck. One of the causes of this was pressure on the operators to occupy themselves primarily with the transmission of messages of a private nature, since the primary function of the radiotelegraph operators was to send personal messages to the passengers. The satisfaction of their clients was a priority for White Star.

Throughout the day, messages from the passengers had been accumulating that needed to be sent out as soon as possible. But the operators did not have much time to do so, given that the transmissions to land could only be done when they found themselves navigating near a radio station, as was the case of the *Titanic* on the afternoon of the accident. As the radiotelegraph operators were conscious that they would end up losing the possibility of sending more messages to land, they occupied themselves fully with this task.

In this context of additional workload, the messages from other boats warning of the presence of icebergs were ignored. As a result, the operator of the boat that sent the last warning, the *Californian*, was reprimanded impolitely by the radiotelegraph operator of the *Titanic*, who asked that they not bother them anymore since they were fully occupied. If the priority of the radiotelegraph operators had been security instead of the satisfaction of passengers, the telegraph wouldn´t have been used for the passengers´ private messages and would have been used for messages of alert that were coming in. *Priorities mark our decisions and our actions, and for this reason we need prioritize correctly, in order to decide and act correctly.*

* * *

In *Alice in Wonderland*, the protagonist finds herself at a crossroads of four paths where she sees a white rabbit who is continually looking at his watch running towards her from far away, constantly repeating "I´m late, I´m late..." When he meets Alice at the crossroads, the animal asks himself with palpable nervousness which path he should take. The girl asks him where he would like to go and the rabbit responds that he doesn´t know. "Well, therefore," says Alice, "it doesn´t matter which road you choose because you will never get there."

This is precisely what happens frequently when we make decisions and do not really know what we want to achieve. If we do not know, it is difficult to reach the goal, and if we do reach it, it will be due to luck. As a result, before making a decision, it is fundamental to previously identify what we would like to achieve. We are accustomed to assuming we know we want, but, a lot of times, it is not like this, and we need to reflect in order to know our true objectives, and sometimes we present questions as problems that are not really so.

The director of a commercial department of a company dedicated to manufacturing computers, decided how he would need to sell the computers. Upon reflection, he realized that the reason that he wished to increase sales was to earn more money and to have a more relaxed life. From there he concluded that what he wished was not to sell more computers, but to have a better quality of life. As a result, he decided to start his own business that allowed him more flexibility in terms of hours.

If this director would have made decisions aimed at increasing computer sales, then achieved this, he still would not have resolved his problem, which was different. Before reflecting on this, he wouldn´t have known it, however. It has to do with analyzing the problem carefully so that the possible solutions that can be reached are really resolved. Reflection about what are our true objectives is what permits us to define them clearly.

And what does it mean to reflect on your objectives? In the first place, it implies asking yourself a simple question. "What do I want or need to achieve?" and responding in writing. Why in writing? Because by noting on paper what our objectives are we can avoid distracting ourselves with the passage of time. Also, we can more easily come back to our initial goals during our reflection process, let things rest, take them up later; that is to say, make considerations.

Additionally, the mere fact of writing them down will provoke one´s mind to think about them, and then ideas related to them will come to us. It is like when one starts thinking about changing one´s car. At the moment that one makes this an objective, one thinks about cars on the street more and starts analyzing. Apart from writing down the objectives, it is a good idea to think about the benefits that one can obtain if one reaches them, and this not only will prompt one to make an effort to reach them but also to see if the benefits outweigh the costs, and, for this, if it makes sense to take them on as objectives.

Finally, once we concretely identify the objectives and evaluate their benefits, we will be able to commit ourselves to achieving them. That is to say, accept them and make ourselves responsible for reaching them. As soon as we have them defined, we must commit ourselves to reaching them. A person can have a diet as an objective, and this is a fundamental decision, but once decided, he or she needs to make an effort to reach his or her goal.

On the other hand, if the objectives we aim to reach are ambitious ones, the decisions we will make to reach them will also be ambitious, and, on the contrary. For this reason, if we give ourselves ambitious goals, we will have more possibilities of achieving results that are meaningful than if we opt for more mediocre objectives. The most relevant decisions are made by people whose objectives imply a greater challenge. If your objective is to end world hunger, though you will not achieve it, you will probably help more people than if your goal is to give the beggar next to your house sweets for Christmas.

Apart from knowing exactly what it is that we would like to achieve, we must also clearly establish and clarify the criteria that will allow us to make one decision or another. The criteria are the elements or the conditions that we require for a decision, that is to say that if for one person, simplicity is a fundamental criterion, then the decision made will need to be simple.

Having clear criteria and explaining them helps us to make decisions and to clarify what we would really like to obtain. If someone needs to make a decision about which of two job offers he or she should accept, and the most important criterion is money for him or her, it will be important to choose the one which offers the most income, but if the criterion is how close the job is to home or the work schedule, it will be important to take the job that is closest to home or the one with the most favorable timetable. In whichever case, what one needs to do is to have clear which are the criteria for making a decision in accordance with his or her real necessities and interests.

What is preferable, also in this case, is to write down the criteria, and once they are written down, they should be listed in order of importance, that is to say, prioritized because some criteria will be given more relevance in order to make decisions than others, and for this it is important to have them clear and organized, so that one does not end up making decisions that do not satisfy one's objectives.

A couple that is expecting their first child has decided to change their car. The criteria that they are using for their decision is that the car is one that they like and, at the same time, is practical. They end up buying an all-terrain vehicle with only two doors, which satisfies their criteria of a car that they like. When they have their child they realize that taking their baby's car seat out of the car every time is a nuisance since the backseat of the car is very small. They end up changing the car because the one they have bought is not practical for them. Since they didn't correctly prioritize their criteria initially, and they gave too much importance to the fact that they would buy a car that they like a lot instead of a practical one, they made a choice that did not make sense for them.

Decision-making criteria and their prioritization have great utility at the moment of making a decision among various possibilities. If we have doubts about whether to buy a house on the outskirts of a city or an apartment in the center, the criteria and their prioritization are a great help when it comes time to decide what to do. If, for example, for us the fundamental criterion is not to have to take a car everywhere, therefore our decision will be to buy the apartment. The choice of criteria and their prioritization is something that only depends on us, but it is unpardonable if we don´t make an effort to clarify them.

SUMMARY OF IDEAS

• Before making a decision, clearly identify what you would like to obtain.

• Think carefully about the objectives you have because these are what will guide you to one decision or another.

• If you set yourself ambitious goals, you may be able to achieve impressive results.

• Don´t wish to have everything, because you will end up with nothing: focus on what is most important for you and forget secondary questions.

• Once you have defined your objectives, you must commit yourself to their achievement.

03.

Frame Your Problems in a Realistic Manner

The *Titanic* was known by most people as "the unsinkable" ship. This aura of indestructibility that surrounded the ship was caused by articles in the principal media of the time, where much reference was made to the impossibility of the ship sinking due to the use of the most technologically advanced methods of the time in its construction. The atmosphere was one of genuine and unbounded confidence, partly due to the fact that the years prior to the sinking were free of any significant disasters within the navigational sphere.

The directors of the shipping company, as well as the technicians involved in the construction of the boat were not immune to this generalized climate of excessive confidence in the real capacities of the vessel. This led them to not put sufficient stress on the control of the fundamental elements for the security of the boat. Why dedicate resources to avoid sinking if the boat was unsinkable?

As the directors had not foreseen the possibility that the boat would sink, they did not find it inconvenient to omit elements destined to mitigate the effects of a possible accident. Hence, they decided to eliminate some lifeboats, as well as to lower the height of some watertight compartments, whose purpose was to prevent the passage of water from one compartment to the next, in the case of a breach in the hull, which would cause the ship to sink. *Their own confidence that sinking of the ship was impossible, led them to ignore the measures to avoid it. Decisions were made on the basis of generalized opinions and not on facts. Euphoria led them to dismiss and not consider the possibility of disaster in a realistic way.*

* * *

The same problem can be seen from very different points of view

31

and the decisions that we make depend on how we view the problem. In an American hospital, they conducted an experiment in which patients with pulmonary cancer had to decide whether or not to undergo surgery. When the situation was presented to them by telling they had a 68% chance of surviving the first year after undergoing surgery, many decided to go through with it. When they were told that despite undergoing surgery, they had a 32% chance of dying the first year after surgery, the majority decided not to have the operation.

Some real estate agents play with this fact when a client comes in to buy an apartment. First, they show the client an ugly and expensive apartment, the second one they show is also ugly and expensive. The buyer starts to get anxious. The third one they are shown – the one that in reality the agent would like to sell –is a normal apartment at a normal price (if there are normal apartments at normal prices), so that they decide to take it immediately, as it is a jewel when compared to the prior apartments. If they would have shown this apartment at the beginning as the first alternative, the clients would not have seen it with the same positive eyes that they see it now.

In one U.S. state, there existed a law they made it obligatory for all cars to have limited liability insurance; additionally, all clients could also take out fire insurance, as well protection for airbag failure buy paying a supplementary premium. The majority of car owners would not pay that additional premium. Nevertheless, in a neighboring state, the fire insurance and protection against airbag failure were already included in the initial price of the insurance. If clients did not want this additional coverage, they could then opt out and get a reduction in the premium paid. In this state, the majority of drivers did not ask for the reduction in insurance coverage. These cases bring us back to the fact that the same situation, presented in one way or another, leads to distinct decision-making.

The following experiment also confirms this fact. A group of people were told they could buy a computer for one thousand euros, but that if they went to a store that was 20 minutes away on foot, they could obtain the exact same computer, but for a reduced cost of 988 euros. The majority of them decided not to walk those 20 minutes and bought the one thousand euro computer.

Another group of people was told that they could buy a calculator for 30 euros, but if they walked for 20 minutes they could find the same calculator for sale at a different store for only 18 euros. In this case, the majority of people decided to walk 20 minutes and buy the cheaper calculator. In reality, all of the participants were being asked the very same question, "Would you walk 20 minutes to save 12 euros?" In another light, the response was distinct depending on the context in which the question was posed (given either spending one thousand euros or 30 euros).

In this case, the observation is made that people reason in relative terms: computer buyers were barely saving 1% by waking 20 minutes, whereas those buying a calculator were saving 40%. But when one saves money, one is saving money in concrete terms and not in percentages and, therefore, the decision must be made with absolute savings in mind and not based on relative savings. This is a case that that shows that framing problems in an adequate manner leads to better decision making.

Considering a problem in a realistic way basically consists of focusing on the root of the problem, that is to say, asking oneself what primary causes are provoking the problem. If person has a headache, that person can take an aspirin to alleviate the pain. But if the cause of the pain is that he or she has bad nutritional habits, then taking an aspirin does not resolve these difficulties, just the symptoms. In order to resolve these difficulties in an effective manner, the person may need to adjust his or her diet. In this case, adjusting one's dietary habits implies going to the root of the problem, while taking an aspirin only resolves the symptoms that continue to appear until the root of the problem is sorted out.

One frequent form of not adequately considering problems is to define them in terms of solutions, in other words by, placing emphasis on one possible solution to the problem. Let's look at an example: An overworked warehouse manager tells his boss, "We have a problem at the warehouse, we need more workers". With this presentation of the problem, there is no possibility for analysis because when bringing up the problem a solution is presented (hiring more employees).

Nevertheless, if we present the same problem by pointing out the actual facts that may be causing it—"the warehouse work orders are not coming out on time"— then, aside from the lack of personnel, other alternative solutions can be considered to resolve the problem, like the organization of work, as well as materials, and work processes and methods... When we include a solution while declaring the problem, the analysis of other possible solutions is limited.

Considering problems in an advantageous manner also implies doing so realistically. The extent to which we consider problems realistically allows us to have more possibilities to make correct decisions. The difficulty lies in the subjective perception of reality, that is to say, the biases held by the one who is considering the problem. This explains the fact that, for example, for some people one determined presidential candidate is best suited to lead a nation, while for other people, the most suitable person will be someone else. Each one of us has our particular vision of reality that conforms to our experiences, education and personality. The perception or reality is subjective and each person sees situations in a distinct manner.

Given the subjective bias through which we look at reality, considering problems in a realistic manner also implies that we differentiate between facts and opinions. One thing is the reality (the facts) and another thing is the subjective perception of that reality. Discerning between either of these improves the efficacy of making decisions. Stating that product X has lost 20% of its market share is a fact, but saying the product is obsolete may be a value judgment. Perhaps the product is just as attractive in and of itself, but distributors, for example, no longer have an interest in selling it because other products are more profitable to sell.

If we focus on the facts, or on what is happening in reality, and this is ascertainable, then we can consider problems in a realistic way, and avoid personal biases. To consider a problem and make a decision, it is necessary to focus on the facts, on what has actually happened and not on the opinions or interpretations of these facts.

In addition, optimism and pessimism allow us to consider problems better. If we are excessively optimistic or pessimistic, our perception of reality will be biased, making it more difficult to consider situations realistically. Another frequent error made when considering problems is to focus on finding culprits, rather than on seeing how to solve the problem at its source. Looking for blameworthy targets does not help us to resolve problems.

SUMMARY OF IDEAS

• If you do not consider the possibility of something happening, then you cannot take precautionary measures so that it does not occur.

• If you declare problems while including a solution, then you limit the possible alternative solutions.

• Focus on the facts and not on opinions to effectively consider problems.

• Considering problems in a realistic manner means asking oneself what root causes are provoking these problems.

• Resolve your problems without getting hooked solely on searching for someone or something to blame.

04.

Do Not Deceive Yourself,
It's Very Easy To Do This

During the construction of the *Titanic*, decisions were made that compromised its own security: The first of these decisions was the number of lifeboats incorporated, and the second dealt with the height of the ship's compartments. Let's examine the first. The cause of the sinking was the collision with the iceberg, but it was the insufficient number of lifeboats on board that led this disaster to result in a tragedy. Had there been space for everyone, many deaths could have been avoided. But, why weren't there enough lifeboats on board?

The initial plan, during the design of the vessel, was to place sixty-four lifeboats on board, enough for all of the passengers. This number was reduced to twenty because this resulted in better ocean views from the deck. Since the final objective was to build a luxury ship, security elements became secondary. With twenty boats instead of the necessary sixty-four, in the case of sinking, the loss of life would be greater than it otherwise could have been.

In any case, the ship complied with the observed rules. According to the law, a vessel like the *Titanic* was obligated to carry sixteen lifeboats. But, in the world of navigation, it was generally accepted knowledge that the number of lifeboats required by law was insufficient to evacuate the passengers in the case of an accident. In fact, the British maritime authorities had, on various occasions, attempted to change the law, but they always encountered strong opposition from the builders who were conscious that placing more lifeboats on board implied greater costs.

Before accepting the sure cost of adding lifeboats, it was preferable to decrease the number of boats, trusting that these would never be necessary. White Star directors defended their decision about the number of boats based on the fact that with only twenty lifeboats, the *Titanic* met the legal requirement that they knew was obsolete. Therefore, they found a perfect excuse to justify something that they knew would place hundreds of human lives in danger. In the end, they did nothing more than deceive themselves, that is, find a pretext to justify a decision that is difficult to justify.

The second decision that compromised the security of the ship was setting the height of the compartments. The company directors, who were above all concerned with luxury, repeatedly insisted to the architects that the communal spaces, and especially the restaurants and salons, be spacious. But, in order to attain these required dimensions, the engineers had to compromise another initially anticipated element of security: the vessel's compartments.

The boat was initially designed to include sixteen watertight compartments separated by hatches, which served to keep water entering one compartment from passing into another. In the case of an accident, the hatches would prevent the entire area of the boat from being filled with water and sinking. But, when the ship's directors pressured the architects about more spacious salons, it was then necessary to reduce the hatches so that four of them were constructed with only ten feet of height above the flotation line. This meant that, in the case of an accident, water would rapidly cover all the inferior compartments and the boat would sink sooner, without time for the a properly organized evacuation of passengers.

The ship's directors prioritized luxury over security in their decisions. That is to say, they renounced something in itself impossible to renounce. And this was possible because they probably did not have it clear that security was an element with little margin for negotiation. Had they been conscious that security was something impossible to abandon, they would not have compromised it so much. The best way to avoid this form of self-deception is to be clear about what the priorities are from the beginning, because if not, important matters such as security, can easily be overlooked.

* * *

Often, when making decisions, before analyzing the distinct alternatives and openly reasoning which is the most advisable, we opt for one of the alternatives for emotional reasons or because we have an intuition that the alternative is better.

At that moment, closing out the consideration of other possibilities is a common error. George Bush decided to invade Iraq due to certain motives at the time. Once the decision was made all there was left to do was to find a cause to justify it. The excuse that Iraq was producing weapons of mass destruction served as an argument to initiate war. But this was simply the pretext to initiate the invasion that had already been decided on beforehand, without analyzing the consequences nor other possible alternatives.

In a situation such as this, not much attention is paid to the arguments that go against the decision that has already been made. We do not do this because it will not help validate our decision. The information on the absence of weapons of mass destruction was not taken into account. Going against the grain on a decision that has already been made is unpleasant. On the contrary, the reasons that validate the decision already made are usually taken into account. In this manner, many errors are committed.

When we have made a decision, it is difficult for us to change it although there may exist weighty reasons to do so. The most intelligent way to confront a situation of this type is to act as a devil's advocate for the alternative that appears most appropriate. If we opt for an alternative, we should seek out all of the arguments that could show that said option is not the most beneficial.

This way of proceeding assures that all the pros and cons of the distinct alternatives for every decision have been studied; it guarantees that diverse possibilities have been examined, and that the entire affair has been studied from various points of view.

On the 30th of August, 2005, Hurricane Katrina demolished the city of New Orleans in the state of Louisiana. A plan that was elaborated in 1998 called, "Coast 2050", indicated how to proceed in case a hurricane struck the city. It was a plan that could have saved the city. Nevertheless, the Federal Emergency Management Agency (FEMA) did not implement it. The principals in charge of FEMA lacked experience in managing disasters. In reality, they had less experience than what they had claimed on their CVs. The director of the agency affirmed on his official resumé that he had been the municipal manager responsible for emergency services in the city of Oklahoma from 1975 to 1978. However, according to the spokesperson of the municipal government of Oklahoma, he had simply been an assistant to the manager – a type of intern.

Moreover, three of the principal directors of FEMA had obtained their posts after having actively participated in George Bush's 2000 electoral campaign. Meanwhile, two other independent experts with ample experience in disaster management had left FEMA in the years before the Katrina disaster. The members of the commission who were left did not have enough experience, but they did have political connections to the President of the United States. When a superior surrounds him or herself with friends and admirers who always want to be in agreement, problems are avoided. But when difficulties appear, and what is missing are people with the capacity to resolve these problems in an efficient manner, though admirers may still abound, the lack of such individuals can create greater problems.

The competent collaborators with independent opinions that could contradict those of the boss end up being replaced or frustrated that they were never appreciated. The end result is always the same. All possible discussion of appropriate alternatives is ignored and the decision-making process ends up being impoverished due to the lack of open and calm discussion about the advantages and disadvantages of various alternatives. If we listen to the people who surround us and take into account their stances, our capacity to make decisions will be enhanced by their support. On the contrary, surrounding oneself with "idiots" is one way of deceiving oneself.

It's a recognized fact that the psychological impact that an unpleasant situation produces is larger than the positive impact that an equivalent positive situation produces. A 100 euro fine produces in a us a more unpleasant sensation than the pleasure of winning a 100 euro prize in a raffle.

For this reason, when people face an agreeable situation, they enjoy it and they do not make much of an effort to improve it. The good things in our situation only moderately impact on our level of satisfaction. On the contrary, an unpleasant situation has such an impact on us that we will do whatever we can to get out of it. And this sometimes leads us to make decisions that correct the current negative situation, but which involve a risk that is many times excessive. Things may end up fine in the end and, in this case, there is no problem, but they can also go wrong and then lead us to a situation far worse then the previous one.

Enron played the leading role in the largest securities fraud scandal in corporate history. When the managers at Arthur Andersen—the company auditing Enron— realized that the corporation's problems could come to the surface, rather than accept their own guilt, they made a very risky move: to destroy all of the company's documents. What they achieved was not only the loss of their jobs, but also the demise of the legendary auditing firm. This is another indication that when we face painful situations, we make decisions of high risk with consequences that are much more devastating than if we had accepted the initial situation.

President Bill Clinton faced a moment in front of television cameras when he had to inform the public about his relations with an intern. Accepting the reality would have been far too difficult for him. There was a more honorable exit, in his opinion. He decided to lie and say that there had only been a professional relationship between him and his intern, perhaps a bit intense at moments, but nothing more. This decision could have led to desirable results, but it was very risky. And, it ended badly. In the end, the truth came out. It became known that his relationship with the intern had gone farther than a professional relationship. It became known that he had lied to his family and to the American people in front of cameras. Facing a negative situation, Clinton preferred to choose an alternative that would have allowed him to come out on top. The problem was that the alternative was far too risky and had many possibilities of ending in a worse situation than the one he was attempting to avoid.

A similar situation happens to people who invest in the stock market. If the shares in which they have invested go up in value within a reasonable amount of time, they can sell the shares, reaping the profits and exiting happily. On the contrary, if these shares lose partial value, nobody sells. Selling would signify recognizing a loss of one's assets, and this is painful. It is preferable to hold on to the shares, waiting for them to appreciate in value, so that a loss of assets never materializes. Stockholders hold out to see to see if they can avoid the loss of money that buying the shares entailed. The ulterior motive for this behavior is that psychologically, loss occurs when the shares are sold. By not selling the shares, the intention is to avoid this loss. But this is a deception. The real loss—not the psychological one—is produced when the shares lose their value, sold or not. When someone goes to a casino, they go home very happy if they win some money, but if they lose, they do not go home sad, as they should. The person does not want to accept this situation and begins to place more bets to recoup their losses, and normally ends up spending more than what he or she had initially allowed him or herself to lose.

The case of the launch of the space shuttle Challenger also pertains to this paradigm about not accepting a negative situation and fostering self-deception in this action. For some time, the date and time of the launch had been anticipated. On the day of launch, new doubts emerged about whether the low temperatures that were registering would place the security of the spaceship in danger. But they were that: doubts. Postponing the launch would be a sure loss: the entire country was waiting, President Reagan would need to be informed, etc. And, it was not clear that the temperature would influence the success or failure of the launch. Considering this, preference was given to taking the risk of launching before accepting the embarrassing situation of having to postpone the date of the launch.

The same thing happens to mountain climbers who try to climb Mount Everest. There is a rule that states that climbers should give up and descend if the peak has not been reached by 11 in the morning on the last day of the expedition. What does an expedition that has been preparing its ascent during a span of a few years, and that is being sponsored by local banks in the country, do? Television news is covering the expedition, and everyone is waiting for the ascent to the summit and the climbers are thrilled with their exploit.

The last day of climbing arrives and, at 11am, they calculate that there is still one hour left before the summit. What do they do? Well, the most human thing to do is to deceive themselves and continue so as to not disappoint themselves or their country, which is following this event with real emotion. Perhaps nothing will happen, but perhaps something will happen. In any case, it is an excessive risk.

This phenomenon also often causes managers to maintain company projects that are not good. One director makes a decision, and the matter ends badly. In these cases, it is very common that instead of retiring and recognizing that things have gone badly, the director continues to invest money into the project thinking that with a financial injection, the project will be resuscitated and generate revenue. This is normally a form of self-deception. It is refusing to admit that a project that one has decided to invest in is a failure. Recognizing this is very difficult for a manager. And self-deception occurs by rationalizing that with extra investments, the business will turn around. The reality is that money will continue to be lost, and the more the project is financed, the more money that will be lost. It is best to exit this process as soon as possible and recognize that the project has gone awry. Peter Drucker recommended that all managers have periodical meetings within their companies to decide which projects to continue and which investments to abandon. When one has dug him or herself into a hole, the most rational thing to do is to stop digging.

If one finds him or herself in an unpleasant situation, he or she should intend to exit it. In order to do so, he or she should seek alternatives and analyze their consequences, compare each alternative with the current situation, and only when he or she believes that he or she has a better option than the current one, should he or she make a decision to change. But making a change because one's current situation is bad is something that is very risky. Normally, the new situation tends to be worse.

Additionally, when we evaluate the alternative situation in order to compare it to the current one, we should take into account that we very frequently magnify the advantages of the alternative situation and we minimize its inconveniences. And, on the contrary, we tend to exaggerate the negative aspects of our current situation and not pay attention to its positive aspects.

SUMMARY OF IDEAS

• It is costly to change a decision once you have made it, though there may exist weighty reasons to do so.

• Do not make a risky decision just to get out of an unpleasant situation because it is very probable that, in the long-run, you may exit more damaged.

• If you have made an erroneous decision, do not persist with it. It's more practical to recognize the error and modify the decision.

• You will always be able to find pretexts to justify your decisions, but rarely is this more than a form of self-deception.

• *The best way to avoid self-deception is to know what your priorities are, because, if not, you may end up sacrificing your priorities.*

05.

Only Pay Attention To Relevant Information

Before the accident that provoked the sinking of the *Titanic*, many things occurred that could have alerted the captain about the real danger they were up against, but he ignored these, or, at the very least, he did not react in a significant manner in response to the danger. The first thing that happened, that we have already made reference to earlier, were the countless messages that were received alerting the ship of the presence of icebergs in the zone through which the vessel was about to pass. The second issue refers to the temperature drop in the atmosphere, caused by the presence of large masses of ice nearby.

Let's look at the first group of signals to which little attention was paid. During the days before the accident, many messages were received from various ships warning of the existence of icebergs on the *Titanic's* route. Just the day before, Saturday, the 13th of April, at least two more messages arrived with the same message, as well as the signals that the *Rappahannock* steamship had made to them: that while passing next to the *Titanic*, warned them that it had been damaged while traversing the ice floes.

The same day as the accident, the 14th of April, the telegraphic messages that arrived were numerous and largely ignored by the officials on the ship. At 9am, the first warning from the *Caronia*, another vessel, arrived. At 11:40 am, a second warning, from the *Noordam*, arrived. Just after at 2 pm, a message from the *Baltic* arrived. These 3 messages were delivered to the officials on deck by the radio operators. Three minutes after the last message arrived, another message from the *America* arrived, warning, just like all of the others, of the presence of blocks of ice on the *Titanic's* route. This warning was not delivered to the ship's control deck. The fifth message arrived at 7:30 pm, from the *Californian*. This notice was also not delivered to the captain's deck. The last known message, sent by the *Mesaba*, at

9:40pm, just before the collision, was also not delivered to the captain, who at that hour could already be found resting in his cabin. The second group of signals that the officials ignored in a continuous manner relate to the progressive decline in the atmospheric temperature, a clear indicator that the ship was approaching a zone with a lot of ice. Within two hours, the air temperature descended 10 degrees, and at around 7:30pm, it was hovering at around zero degrees Celsius. Similarly, the water temperature also declined significantly, and at 8:30pm, its temperature was also close to zero degrees.

After 9 pm, the captain headed to the control deck before going to bed. There, he spoke to the officer on duty about the meteorological changes, but he did not order the ship to reduce its speed, nor to alter its path significantly, knowing that during a moonless night, such as was the case, it would be very difficult to spot icebergs with enough time to avoid a collision.

The largest question will always be: Why did the captain not react to the countless danger signals that he received? That is, why did he maintain everything the same when danger was imminent? One very probable response is that the objective of the person responsible for the ship was to arrive one day before expected, exerting pressure on the captain to ignore the clear warning signs. Since, had he taken these signals into account, he would have made decisions such as reducing the ship's velocity, which would have made achieving the objective of arriving one day early much more difficult.

In fact, it is customary to ignore signals that we get from reality when these signals contradict our interests, although it is advisable to act cautiously with respect to these same signals. *We filter the information that we receive so that it accommodates our interests, and this causes us difficulty in making decisions that are right for the situation that exists in reality.*

As we have already pointed out, radio operators relayed the three primary messages that reached the ship that warned of the presence of icebergs, to the control deck; however, it is not clear whether the

46

rest were delivered. Why did they stop delivering such warnings? One of the reasons is that formal procedures were not in place regarding what they had to do with warnings that arrived, in which case, what they did with them was left up to their own discretion about what they thought was most appropriate at each moment given their criteria. They had to decide whether the messages were important or not.

The only existing rule was that they needed to communicate to the officer on duty whatever messages that arrived preceded by the code MSG or SOS (both of which indicated the existence of danger). Because the alert messages received did not have said code, they did not consider it obligatory to relay the message. In this situation, the lack of clarity in procedures led to a situation where the relevant information for making decisions, like these alert messages, did not reach the person in charge of deciding, and so, *without clear processes or established channels of communication, it is very difficult for all of the relevant information for decision-making to reach the "decision-maker".*

If the rest of the messages had reached the captain, perhaps he would have been able to react in a different manner, demonstrating more preparation, and although this may not have modified his decision, at the very least he would have known all of the information necessary to make it. The most lamentable part of this situation is that having received key information on multiple occasions, they still made decisions without taking into account this information.

The collision was not very sudden, and this led the control deck to believe that the damage had not been significant, and the rest of the crew and the passengers to perceive that nothing was out of the ordinary, aside from a light beating. As expected, the passengers continued with their normal activities: the majority of them were sleeping and others could be found throughout the various salons. Those who asked the waiters about what had happened received the response of, "nothing alarming". In fact, the crew was convinced that everything was fine. But the point of view from the ship's engine quarters, where the impact was made, was very different. There the water started to come in rapidly, filling the airtight compartments of the ship. The personnel in this area realized that the boat would not remain afloat for long.

Those who were close to the point of impact and could see its effects had a realistic vision of the actual consequences of the crash. In any case, the officers in charge, as well as the crew and passengers, could not fully understand the situation in which they found themselves as they were in a distant location. Consequently, they could not react in a manner adequate to attempt to minimize it. And so, *the perspective from which we see things determines the type of information that we obtain; therefore, it is convenient to analyze distinct perspectives for one situation so as to obtain more information.*

After the collision, the officer on duty ordered that the captain be awakened. The captain who then sent a group of people to perform reconnaissance on the damage suffered. This group took 15 minutes to bring their first impressions to the ship's command deck. Immediately after, the captain, along with the ship's architect, Thomas Andrews, went to personally evaluate the damage.

At that moment, Andrews realized that the crash had damaged six compartments, and that, because the ship was designed to stay afloat with a maximum of four flooded compartments out of the sixteen existing ones, that sinking was inevitable. He speculated at that moment that within space of a couple hours, sinking was inevitable. Now, he had the information necessary to understand with scientific certainty his fatal destiny and to start to make decisions necessary to attempt to avoid a tragedy. However, had they evaluated the damage upon collision, they would have won some precious time to organize the evacuation. If the captain and the architect had made the first reconnaissance of the damages, more people could have been saved, because *until the information is not available from the source, that is to say, understanding of the state of the situation, appropriate decisions cannot be taken.*

So as to not propagate panic, those in charge of the ship decided to try to trasmit to the passengers and to the crew a sensation of absolute normalcy. In fact, the orchestra, led by Wallace Hartley, was asked to continue playing animated songs in order to entertain the people, an activity that they carried out until just before sinking, so that all of the orchestra's members died.

In this context, that is to say, without the crew nor the passengers fully aware of the gravity of the situation, whichever emergency plan that the captain would have proposed to implement would inevitably be limited in its effectiveness. And so when we do not adequately communicate, the reactions of the rest of those affected are also not adequate. This strategy of pseudo-communication, or of occulting the reality, made it difficult for passengers and the crew to be able react with more time so as to make a more effective and overall less hasty evacuation. *Hiding relevant information impeded the effective evacuation of the ship.*

The ship that first arrived at the scene of the accident was the *Carpathia*. This ship was 58 miles from the *Titanic* at the moment that it received the first emergency call at 12:25am. The ship's captain, Arthur Rostron, despite for a moment doubting the message, changed its route in the direction of the Titanic, directing itself towards its rescue.

If you compare the reaction of the *Carpathia's* captain with the *Californian's* captain, which we will analyze further along, a great difference can be observed. The first, upon the first indication of danger, launches itself to the rescue with all means possible, even before checking the actual situation of the ship, while the second ship, after encountering the danger signals, seeks to make sure that the Titanic is actually in hardship, without going to its rescue.

The captain of the *Californian*, in contrast to Rostron, thought too much before acting; he needed too much information to make a decision, and this caused consequences that can be quantified in the number of victims. Nevertheless, the decision and actions of the *Carpathia*, led it to react efficiently. *Sometimes, in situations in which the response time is a fundamental factor, first, it is necessary to act before stopping to obtain more information.*

* * *

The officers need to take decisions in relation to the information that is available to them. The more information they have, the less uncertainty that they will have and the more they can be assured that the results of their decisions will be satisfactory. It is because of this that the officers intend to always seek more information in order to decide, and the more there is, the better. Indeed, the information can be valuable, but it also has a cost. Before seeking information, it is necessary to be certain that the information is useful, and that the cost not be superior than the value it adds.

One example will help clarify these points. A company's account manger was thinking about introducing a new artificially sweetened yogurt without sugar. Making sure this was a good decision was important because the major or minor success of the new product was dependent on it. If he decided go forward with the yogurt that would be well accepted by consumers, the expected benefits would be four million Euros, and if he was mistaken the benefits would be reduced to three million. In circumstances such as these, more than one million euros should never be paid to a company for market research to examine what people's actual preferences are.

The numbers stated in the example above are not realistic, but they illustrate errors that managers frequently make. A manager knows what a market research company will charge him or her for a specific report, but rarely does a manager worry about quantifying the benefits that will be received once he or she has the information. So it is not usual to compare if the cost of the information is superior or not to the value that it provides.

Other times, the cost of information is much less clear, it may not be a bill that is paid to a market research company. This occurs when an internal report is requested within a company. It is fast to request a report, but the hidden costs that its production entails to the people within the company are not generally taken into account. This way, studies are often undertaken in which the actual costs entailed are not known, nor is the value-added of the content known. It is true that the manager is very pleased to make decisions with plenty of information at hand.

Frequently, a company circulates monthly or trimesterly reports that support information that is absolutely irrelevant for the decisions that need to be taken periodically. The reason is that in any given moment within the company there had to have been a series of decisions that were taken, for which it has been necessary to receive certain information. These reports are still produced in a routine way, though they are no longer necessary. Nobody knows why they are produced, everyone things that there must be a reason for it and they keep doing it though it is no longer useful for anyone.

During the time period in which there was no online gambling and there were only pools to bet for the football results, very value information for people (on the other hand impossible to know beforehand) was to know the results of each match, and if the winner would be the local team, the visiting team or if there would be a tie. That is to say, the relevant information was whether in the corresponding shift one needed to be able to choose a 1, an X or a 2. With this information, it was possible to win a lot of money. However, there was nobody who was willing to pay a single euro more to know, additional to which team would win or if they would tie, the concrete results of each match. This information in that time period served for nothing. It is a different thing altogether now that there is online betting on all types of things, an now this information could be very relevant.

That is to say, that at the time when looking for information it is necessary to first ask if the information that is being sought has a value or not. And supposing that it has value for the decisions that need to be taken, it is necessary to prove if this is truly superior or not than the cost of obtaining that information, in which case it is not worth the trouble to search for it.

Another error that is often committed is that that while using the information to make a decision, the information used is that which is available, but not relevante for that situation. In the launching of the challenger space shuttle by NASA in 1985, which we references earlier, it was known that there were small rings that protected the joints of the distinct parts of the motor for all the rockets that did not end up functioning correctly. They had done pilot tests and, on various occasions, these rings had failed. A scientist from NASA warned that these failed when the rocket was launched during cold temperatures. Those responsible for the launching paid not attention, now that the rings had failed when the experiments had been performed at high temperatures, just like in low temperatures, so that they did not thing that the temperatures and the problem of these small rings had any relation.

This is a typical example of the use of available information in place of relevant information. If the data on the temperatures during the pilot experiments had been taken into account, and not only the temperature data in those experiments when the rocket failed, one could have observed that in all of the tests carried out when the temperatures was under 61 degrees F, the rings had failed, meanwhile , they had only failed in very few cases in those experiments carried out when the temperatures was superior to 61 degrees F.

The day on which the Challenger was launched, the temperature was at 36 degrees F. It was very risky to launch it. Nevertheless, it was done. In taking this decision they utilized the information available (temperatures of the pilot launches in which there were failings with the rings), instead of using the relevant information (temperatures of all of the pilot launches).

Many times we collect useful information, but this ends up being excessive. When this happens, we have to prioritize the information that we are going to analyze and which information we are going to dismiss, because when we have too much information and we over-analyze it, it becomes difficult at decision-making time.

Another common error related to information is when we do not collect all of the relevant information about a fact, including having it "at hand". This is what happened in the 9/11 attacks. The intelligence agencies in the United States knew that an important terrorit act involving civil aviation was imminent, yet still, they did nothing. How could this happen? Well the reason is very simple. In the first place, there was a sentiment of invulnerability and dominance in the part of the United States. Just like with the Titanic, the general sentiment was of an invincible country, and much more on American soil. In second place, and this was the technical reason for the attacks on the twin towers on September 11th, 2001, although all of the information was available, it was also dispersed.

There was not once single federal agency or intelligence service that had gathered all of the dtata and centralized the information. Some services alerted that fundamentalists muslims were enrolling themselves in federal pilot academies: other services detected emails that warned about attack plans, and in this way, mountains of diverse pieces of dates existed. So what was the problem? Well, that nobody had aggregated all of the information that would have permitted the failure of those terrible attacks.

Frequently, in the use of information, as we have said previously, there is a tendency to confuse and mix the facts that are judged as valuable, which makes it difficult to properly use this information and make correct decisions. That sales have come down by 10% in the last year is a fact, but whether the cause for this decline is the sales director's performance is value judgment. If, in this case, we take the value judgment as if it were to be a fact, then the decision we are making would have to be the dismissal of the sales director, when perhaps his performance was very efficient and had he not managed as he had, sales would have come down 20% instead of 10%, and firing him would mean making a bad decision.

There exists a certain tendency to convert our opinions into data, real facts, when they are not more than merely opinions. That behavior leads to making bad decisions. Distinguishing between what the facts are and what are merely value judgments leads us to make better decisions.

Finally, as we have already noted, it sometimes happens that before making a decision we choose an alternative before examining the information. It is then that we have a tendency to analyze said information in a biased way. If we choose an alternative before examining the information that is available, when it is done, we may review it in a biased way.

SUMMARY OF IDEAS

• At the hour of looking information, ascertain that its utility is superior to its cost and pay attention to relevant information, not only that which is available.

• Prioritize information because making decisions when having too much information makes it difficult to so the same.

• Clearly distinguish between the part of the information that is comprised of facts and the part that contains value judgments.

• Do not choose an alternative before examining the information.

• *Triumph over the temptation to dismiss relevant information that reaches you, simply because it contradicts your interests. If you deny this information, you will not be able to make decisions that are appropriate for reality.*

06.

Recognize Uncertainty and Manage It

Captain Smith, himself, steeped in the ship's aura of indestructibility, declared in a newspaper of the time that modern ships were constructed in such a manner that their sinking was impossible. From this perspective of excessive confidence, it is not surprising that the captain did not vary the route much nor reduce the ship's speed, despite numerous warnings about icebergs.

He was so confident in the indestructibility of the ship that this assumption influenced, in a determinate manner, the decisions that he made. On the contrary, maintaining skepticism about the assumptions themselves permits us to review a situation at all moments and make better decisions.

Even if initially the plan had been to use the best means and resources for the construction of the ship, as we can see, over the duration of its construction many of these plans were compromised and revised. According to the original design, perhaps the ship was truly "unsinkable", but the initial plan required that many modifications be made that considerably diminished security.

The result is that the aura of indestructibility remained, but not the security elements that supported it. If the designers had critically examined why the ship was considered to be indestructible, they would have realized that there were no longer reasons to support this view. *In order to correctly decide, it is necessary to analyze the assumptions made; it may be that there is nothing to uphold them, and then the decision does not fulfill the expectations.*

* * *

We live in a world in which we never know what is going to happen.

Although we may not like it, uncertainty is a reality. We probably prefer to make decisions knowing beforehand if they are correct or not, but this is a risk we have to take. This situation produces anguish, and because we do not want to live with anguish, we avoid acknowledging that uncertainty exists. But a decision almost always implies some uncertainty and however one wants to avoid this, one ends up negating his or her capacity for making decisions. Whoever is excessively fearful of uncertainty complicates the possibility of making decisions.

Before an uncertain future situation, the first thing we can do is to suppose which is the scenario that is most likely. This assumption is fine as a point of departure, but the error will come subsequently. We believe that the scenario is what it will actually be and we act accordingly, forgetting that things can go differently— in a way much differently than what we have imagined. This is why it is possible that we end up complaining about things that happen in a way opposite from what we had thought.

The examples of the mismanagement of Hurricane Katrina, like the Enron affair, show us that those responsible did not correctly calibrate uncertainties. Imagine a favorable scenario. We try very much to produce this scenario and we forget that things can happen differently from what we had foreseen. The Enron executives became enthusiastic about the possibility of becoming rich, and they did not contemplate the possibility of ending up in prison. Those responsible for disaster management did not want to contemplate the possibility of a hurricane drowning New Orleans when that scenario was scientifically plausible. The *Titanic* directors did not want to contemplate the possibility of crashing into an iceberg.

Wouldn't it be more reasonable to recognize uncertainty beforehand and think about different possible scenarios, some more probable than others? Yes, it is more reasonable, but also it is more complicated and we do not know how to act facing distinct possible futures. It is easier to assume one future and act in agreement with that belief. A false sense of security is very comfortable. The problem is that it is false. But, the advantage is that it is very comfortable. The uncertainty of not knowing what is going to happen worries us. Furthermore, we do not know how to face it. We prefer to assume that there is less uncertainty than there really is. Often, we assume this only to obtain a false appearance of security.

The assumptions that we make about a situation sometimes appear to be so elementary that we fail to question them. This is something that happens to us frequently – that we take for "certain" things that are not so certain – which later leads us to make incorrect decisions. A high-level director of IBM, at one moment, stopped the entry of the company in the business of personal computers because he was convinced that "there was no reason for someone to want to have a computer at home". Another executive of cinematography studies caused his company to encounter business difficulties because he was convinced that "people did not want to hear actors speak in films". And, the same year that the Beatles made their debut, a record company director affirmed that "pop groups did not have a future". Seeing these examples, we can come to realize that questioning our own assumptions facilitates our ability to make better decisions.

Diverse experiments made with people demonstrate that we prefer security, although it may be false, to uncertainty. One of these consists of asking a group of people a question at the time that they are given many possible responses. For example, a question asked may be, "How many times has Brazil won the World Football Championship?" They are given two responses to choose from: 4 times or 5 times. It is asked that they first respond if they know the answer with certainty. If they say yes, then they are asked to say so. Logically, within the group of people who know the response with certainty, all of them should give the correct answer, but...this is not the case. There are always 10% to 20% of people who say they are sure of something that ends up being false. Antonio Machado said this in one of his poems: "In my solitude, I have seen things very clearly, that are not true". And this happens in a systematic way. This happens regardless of the question and regardless of what the question may be; to sensible managers, MBA students... unfailingly. In general, when a person says that he or she is sure of something, normally the level of real certainty he or she has is between 80% to 90%.

When we are planning the future of our company, we need to have assumptions. To plan expenditure, production, etc, we need foresight about sales, but also to analyze alternative scenarios. If, for example, we think that the sales of our company in the following year will be 1,000, we analyze the situation in scenarios that include broadly 10% more or less sales, and, in this way, we plan imagining that sales could be 1,000, 900 or 1,100.

Well fine, when we do this we always underestimate the uncertainty. Normally in these cases, the variation in sales can be between 700 and 1,300. What happens is that such a wide range disconcerts us; it makes us think that we are incompetent because we do not know how to predict sales, leaving us not knowing what to do and paralyzing us. This is why we prefer to assume some fluctuations of sales very close to 1,000. But this is an error, because later reality comes with sales of 750 or 1,200 and chaos is produced in the company, and we are left with excessive expenditures or with a level of production far beyond our capacity.

Since we normally underestimate uncertainty and are more sure of how things are going to go than we really should be, it is better to imagine that this can turn out to be very distinct from how we think; and, at the hour of planning, it is also better to make contingency plans just in case those scenarios, in the end, are the ones that in reality are produced, and, in this case, we will be prepared to face an increase or decrease in sales without producing chaos within the company. The questions that we face can be operative or not operative. The operative ones are those where we that have the correct results beforehand, like, for example, calculating the liters of water that come out of a tap during a period of time. The ones that are not operative are those where we do not know if there is a correct solution beforehand, like investing a determined amount of money in one project or another.

Making decisions about operative questions does not represent a real uncertainty, but the questions that are not operative that are the most important decisions, do implicate uncertainty. Furthermore, the sense of doubt can be converted into a sense of oppression because since we were small children we have been educated to make decisions about operative problems, but not about non-operative questions. In school, they show us how to add, but not how to decide what our best professional option will be.

Non-operative problems, which do not have pre-existing solutions, introduce us to the environment of uncertainty because we will never be able to know if the decision we have made was the best one. Well, although it may have functioned well, it may be possible that another decision would have functioned better. Futhermore, this feeling grows because there can be, and there usually is, more than one solution to the same problem. Despite having decided correctly, we will always wonder if we were wise or not.

Normally, we are scared of uncertainty. We do not know how to treat it. But, it's precisely in this uncertainty where opportunities are produced. If the entire world knew beforehand about the results of the lotteries nobody would win money in these games. Let's anticipate uncertainty and incorporate it into our lives. This will get us more prepared and offer opportunities to benefit from this. Whoever accepts doubt, places him or herself at the disposal of being able to benefit from it.

Recognizing uncertainty implies taking risk. A person who is not prepared to take risk, at least a little bit, cannot make quality decisions, or the ones they make will not be very innovative. Every decision is, ultimately, a step into a vacuum, because we do not know the consequences that each step will have. Therefore, whoever is not willing to take risks, will make very few decisions. Moreover, in the actual context of continuous change, what is truly risky is not taking risks at all.

If a racecar driver does not make the decision to pass up his rivals because he can collide with them when doing so, then he will not be able to win the race. If he desires victory, he will have to take a risk. But, the risks should be calculated: the possible negative consequences need to be assumable and they need to generate learning so that the same mistakes are not committed once and again. They interviewed a successful NBA player in a newspaper shortly after he retired, and when they asked him which basket hurt most to fail at in his entire career, he responded, "The one that I didn't dare throw." If uncertainty is not tolerated, there is no risk taken, and if risk is not taken, it will be difficult to obtain important results.

SUMMARY OF IDEAS

• If you excessively fear uncertainty, you will negate your capacity to make good decisions because a decision almost always implies uncertainty.

• In order to decide well, you must be open to assuming risks.

• Excessive confidence makes it impossible to make decisions appropriately, so that you end up taking as "facts" questions that should only be assumptions.

• Critically analyze the assumptions that you make before making a decision; do not let it be the case that there is no support for it, and then the decision will be erroneous.

• *When we make forecasts we have the tendency to underestimate uncertainty.*

07.

Be Creative and Generate Alternatives

The *Californian* was the ship that was closest to the *Titanic* at the moment of the accident, only about 10 miles away. However, it arrived later than the *Carpathia*, which was 58 miles away. When the *Californian* went to the rescue it was already too late. Why did it not go before? Two reasons can explain this delay.

The first is that they had sent two warning messages from the *Californian* to the *Titanic* and they didn't pay any attention in either case: one message was sent at 19:30 and another just before the collision, and where they obtained the famous response from the operator from the *Titanic* asking them to be quiet because he was at work. At that moment, the radio operator of the *Californian*, Cyril Evans, went to bed seeing that his efforts were in vain.

The second reason that she did not go the rescue sooner is that they did not understand the SOS flares that the *Titanic* was sending them. On the *Californian* they saw emergency signals from the transatlantic. When at about 00:00 they saw the first white flare, the officer on duty, Stone, advised his captain, who was resting in his cabin and who told him to try to get in contact with them through the Morse light. After this flare, four others followed in distinct intervals, but the *Californian* continued to insist on the fact that she did not receive a response from the *Titanic*.

During all this time nobody on the *Californian* thought that it was necessary to wake up their telegraphist to get in contact with the *Titanic* through radio to see if they had problems. That is to say, if they had called the operator they would have received information that the ship was sinking and that they needed help, but nobody did that. Instead, *they continued doing the same thing—sending useless signals with the Morse light— without generating effective alternatives.*

* * *

In order to be able to decide we need alternatives. Without these there is no possible election. *Consequently, the more alternatives there are, the better possibility of selection we will have in order to make a decision.* The options give us possibilities at the hour of making a decision. In this way, the generation of alternatives is converted into a fundamental element of making quality decisions.

The director of a company of private jets faced the dilemma about what resolution to take in order to reduce the costs of demonstration to its clients. The options that he was evaluating included making the demonstrations shorter or simply to stop doing them. He didn't know what to do.

Instead of limiting himself to these options, one of his collaborators generated new ones in order to gather more clients in the same demonstrations he used the demonstration so that the client could take a business trip that he already had planned and be able to charge a part of this trip and he took advantage of the contact with the client in the demonstration to try to sell other products and essentially cover the costs of the trip.

With the newly generated alternatives, the director found himself with the possibility of opening up his spectrum at decision making time, and ameliorating the quality because the more alternatives a person is capable of generating, the more possibilities he or she will have to make a good decision. In this sense, creativity acquires important relevance in the decision making process since it permits us to generate alternatives.

Reality indicates to us that there are people with a greater creative capacity than others. But we all have two cerebral hemispheres and, regarding that, we all have rational capacity and creative capacity. The traditional education systems are on track to boost the rational hemisphere, and as a result, we do not use the creative part as much. But the fact that we have a bit of atrophy does not signify that we cannot develop this side, because we still have it. Indeed, even less creatively gifted people can augment it and take advantage of its benefits. Creativity can be fostered. One can be more creative.

The principal problem for developing our creativity usually comes from being our own selves. On the one hand, aspects such as stress, frustration and fear of ridicule incarcerate our creative capacity. Because we do not want to exit the norm, we do not find alternatives to the problems that confront us for fear that others will reject them. It is more secure for our self-esteem not to be unconventional and be more, but this blocks our capacity to generate new ideas.

Lack of confidence in oneself does not only cause us not to be creative, but it also provokes us to always make excuses before about our own selves so as to not make decisions that we think would be good to make. We hide behind reasons such as "I don't have time" or that "It won't work", when in reality we should be telling ourselves: "I am scared". If we liberate ourselves from fear, our decisions will be more creative and more efficient.

On the other hand, we boycott our creativity by behavior in which we go about evaluating the alternatives as we are generating them. Many people do this, that is, make realizations at the same time as in the process of generating ideas and evaluation. The result is that these same people dismiss their alternatives at the same times as they create them. In order to avoid this, it is necessary to separate the process of creating alternatives from the process of evaluating them. That is to say, first we should allow all the ideas that we can think of to come to the forefront, then later, and only later, go about evaluating them one by one: in this way we are able to generate more ideas, and not discard beforehand some which are certainly valid.

The entrepreneurial environment is also not in the custom of fostering creativity. Frequently, it is customary to reject new proposals to continue more or less the same patterns that govern a company. The excuses are always the same: "we do not have a budget"; "we already did something similar and it did not function". This leads, on occasion, to good ideas being rejected.

We have to overcome the brakes that arise from within ourselves, as well as those that arise from exterior factors, in order to be more creative because there is no reason to assume that the first alternative that occurs to us when facing a problem is the best. In relation to that, if we want to make high quality decisions, we have to continue to generate alternatives. Quantity is the sister of creativity, and creativity, of the ability to make correct decisions. Having more alternatives gives us the capacity to choose and those who do not have these, do not choose, they do the only thing they can: follow their only alternative.

People who only have one option are obligated to follow it and defend it no matter what the cost is. There is nothing more dangerous than one idea when it is the only one that one has. It is their only possibility to act, and if one does not follow it, one will not be able to give a response to what it is one wants to solve. The result is that the decisions will be of bad quality because the best option has not been chosen, but rather, the only one has been chosen.

SUMMARY OF IDEAS

• There is nothing more dangerous than an idea when it is the only one that one has: if you generate alternatives, it will be possible to choose, but if you do not, it will not be.

• If you make a decision and it is not giving you the results that you expected, do not continue doing the same thing: generate efficient alternatives that are useful.

• To be more creative, separate the moment of generating alternatives from the time of evaluation.

• Fear paralyzes our creative capacity.

• *If we have a good idea, we cannot dismiss it for fear of what other people will think.*

08.

Take Into Account That Your Decisions Have Consequences

We have seen that the competitive strategy of *White Star* meant constructing a ship of great size. But, in that era, those with previous experience in the construction of ships with the dimensions of the *Titanic*, did not exist. Those constructing the *Titanic* did not really know how those ships would perform, what the advantages were and what their difficulties were. In this sense, the decision to construct ships like this presupposed an elevated level of uncertainty.

The directors of the naval company made a decision, but perhaps they did not fully take into account all of the implications of this decision, one of these being an element relevant to the uncertainty regarding the security on the ship. And, it is the case that the decisions that we make always have consequences, whether we want them to or not. Due to this, before deciding, it is fundamental to analyze the implications that our decisions could have. If we do not do this, we risk the danger that the negative consequences of our decisions surpass the benefits that we are attempting to reach, for not having analyzed the possible consequences of our decisions.

In the case of the builders of the *Titanic,* the decision to build a large ship could have had, as a consequence, diminished security for the passengers. If they had wanted to avoid this possibility, they should have improved their security measures, which they did not do.

Before beginning the inaugural voyage, the plan was to carry out some navigation tests with the crew, but due to unfavorable meteorological conditions, they decided to cancel the trials. Finally, all that they accomplished was a short test run. This reduction was not considered a relevant element seeing as how, as we have already pointed out, the confidence in the security of the ship was elevated. Although the reality was that little experience in the navigation of such large ships was had by anyone, the crew´s experience in working on a ship of this type was practically nonexistent.

Additionally, the crew barely knew each other. In fact, almost everyone boarded two days before the voyage, and the captain boarded just hours before the voyage. The result was that they did not prepare for the crossing, nor were the protocols for action outlined beforehand, nor were the reactionary systems against possible accidents tested. Therefore, when the collision occurred, the rescue procedures had to be improvised, which explains a lot about the inefficiencies that took place during the evacuation.

The lack of rehearsing and practice led those responsible for managing the ship to not be able to react in an adequate manner; on the one hand, to avoid a crash, but on the other hand, to minimize the effects if such a possibility were to occur. *Let's anticipate and be prepared to adequately manage the possible undesired effects of our decisions so as to reduce them.*

Another element related to the contruction of the ship that compromised its security was the election of the type of steel for the hull. The steel used had a high proportion of sulfur and it was considered the best material of its time because it was more resistant to pressure, but at the same time it was a material that had still not been experimented with much, since its use was not very extensive.

The subsequent investigations of the collision demonstrate that the type of steel was not the most adequate, given that upon receiving a dry hit, and, additionally, at lower temperatures, the steel is converted into something almost as vulnerable as glass. If they had used another type of steel commonly used in the era, it is probable that the hull, instead of breaking and permitting water to enter, may have simply been deformed.

The builders of the ship decided to incorporate new elements so that the vessel would have "the best", but these materials had still not been sufficiently checked in practice. They decided to innovate in its construction, but in association with that innovation, elements of control were not put into place, just like tests with regards to the resistance of materials that would minimize possible adverse effects. When deciding to use a type of steel that had not been tried out on the ship's hull, precisely because it was new, they should have carried out all types of tests in all conditions to see if the hull was reliable, minimizing risk. They did not do this and only became aware of the dangers of the composition of the steel when the ship was already sinking. When facing innovative decisions, one should try to avoid a response that has not been anticipated.

The highest ranking officer on the *Californian*, Captain Stanley Lord, in contrast to Smith, maximized the precautionary measures before the warnings they had received, informing them about the presence of blocks of ice on the route. The first thing he did was reduce the ship's speed, and later, when he saw the first icebergs, he ordered the ship to stop until dawn in order to be able to continue the trip with greater visibility.

Facing the same situation and with the same information, the captains of the two ships made distinct decisions. When balancing losses and wins or pros and cons of a decision, Capital Lord placed security at one extreme of the scale and on another extreme, speed, and he opted for the first. Meanwhile, Captain Smith chose the latter when faced with the same situation. The consequences of each of these elections, lamentably, were palpable. *When faced with a decision, it is good to identify what will be won given the choice if things go well, but it is also recommended to identify what can be lost, if things end up badly.*

* * *

We are free to decide what we consider to be the most correct given certain conditioning external factors that we have, but, once we have decided, in a way we lose control of the consequences derived from that decision. The consequences come with the decision.

When the time comes to make decisions, one of the conditioning mental factors of which we have to be conscient and try to avoid, is that we tend to give excessive weight to the consequences that will be produced in the immediate future and we concede little importance to the consequences of futures more distant in time. But we cannot forget that the future always ends up arriving and that reality sets in.

The most paradigmatic example comes from the Bible when Isaac sells his birthright for a plate of lentils. He arrived from war famished and bought from his brother the possibility of satiating his current hunger for an immensely high price: the privileges of his birthright. Isaac valued his actual hunger, and practically did not take into account the cost of instant gratification, as he would pay this price in the future. At the time of weighing the consequences of our decisions, it is necessary to take into account what will result in the short-term, as well as in the long-term.

We make decisions because there are unpleasant situations that we want to disappear, or because, though there may not be an unpleasant situation, we intuit that we can improve something and we attempt to do something in order to achieve it. If, with this decision that we have made, we have resolved the problem that we had, we think that we have decided well, and if the problem is not resolved, then we think we have done something wrong. But things are not so simple. Sometimes we make a decision through which we resolve a problem that we had, but that same decision has certain undesired collateral effects that can generate a larger problem than the one we expected to resolve.

King Midas wanted to be very rich. He had to do something in order to achieve this and decided to ask the goddess Minerva for the ability to be able to convert all things that he touched into gold. The goddess conceded his wish and King Midas resolved his problem, except that... he encountered an even larger problem.

The fable about the boy who cried wolf offers us another example.

The shepherd boy wanted to entertain himself and achieved this by devising a plan to laugh at the youth of his village. The decision to shout, "The wolf is coming!" was efficient. He managed to entertain himself at the expense of others, except that during the third time, when the wolf really came, he encountered a problem that he was unable to resolve.

Kenneth Lay, the president of Enron, had the same problem as King Midas. He wanted to be very rich, and when his company's profit started to weaken, the decision he made was to manipulate Enron's accounting and make it appear that there were profits that, in reality, did not exist. His decision was efficient, and he resolved the problem that he had. He came to be very rich, except that, in the end, the cover was blown and he found himself with an unforeseen problem that was much larger than what he expected to solve. Sometimes, the unwanted consequences of the decisions that we make are worse than what we expected to resolve.

All of these examples have a common base. We consider a decision as correct or not if it resolves the problem that we set out to solve. But this criterion has many weaknesses. The decisions that we make, as mentioned before, aside from solving a problem or not, have other consequences. Concretely, when we make a decision, we need to pay attention to three things:

• Is the problem that we have going to be solved with this decision?

• What impact will this decision have on the people that it affects?

• What impact does this decision have on me?

If we have three aspects of the decision in mind, we shall see that ideas that might have seemed correct, are no longer so, not at all. In the fable of the boy who cried wolf, he accomplished what he set out to do: to have a good time for a short while. And what about the other aspects? What happened to the youth of the town? What happened to the shepherd boy himself? Well, the youth lost confidence in him little by little, until the third time he cried wolf, they did not believe that he needed help and so that is why what happened did. On the other hand, what happened to the shepherd boy is that he ended up becoming a liar and he had to face the wolf himself.

In the same way, the president of Enron, when manipulating the company's accountability, solved his problem: he became richer. But with this manipulation, what happened to the people affected by his decision? In the first place, investors bought company stocks based on fraudulent information about the situation. The employees had their pensions invested in company stocks because they were confident that they were working for a solid company when everything was a lie. And, what happened to Kenneth Lay, himself? Well, he ended up in jail. When we base our decisions solely considering the first aspect—the resolution of the problem—the decision may be the correct one by chance.

In general, a useful criterion when making decisions is to ask oneself: if the people who are affected by this decision knew what my intentions were when making it, would they lose trust in me or not? If the answer is yes, it is better to avoid this decision, although these people never knew what your intentions were. But, why is this so since they will never find out?

We will answer this with an example. Let us imagine that there is a person with a money belt and we do not know exactly how much money he has. Let us suppose that I have the possibility of taking a bill from him without anybody else knowing that I have done this. Furthermore, this person will never know that someone has taken a bill from them because the reality is that he did not know how much money he had. Moreover, I have met this person on a trip on a train, and had never seen this person before nor will see this person again in the future.

Well, if in these circumstances when I take a bill, my decision will be incorrect. Of course, I will have resolved the problem of having more money, and moreover I will never get caught. But, what happens to the person that who was affected by my decision? He will not be able to enjoy the money that is his and that belongs to him. What will happen to me? Well, I will become a thief. My decision, although efficient, does not pass the essential test of good decisions. If the person affected by my decision were to know the underlying intentions of my actions, he will lose trust in me. My decision is incorrect.

In order to make efficient decisions in the long term, we should evaluate the convenience of an alternative considering if the problem we expect to solve is resolved or not, as well as the impact on others and the impact on ourselves. But one thing to keep in mind is the consequences of our decisions on others, and another is to make a condition of the decision what we think others may think about our decisions. This last point can be a brake for appropriate decision making, with the aggravating fact that later the consequences of the decisions that we have made are conditioned by others, although we are the ones living them, not others.

SUMMARY OF IDEAS

• You are free to decide what you want, but once it is done you are not free to choose the consequences of your decision.

• Before making a decision, think about what you can win if things turn out well, but also about what you can lose, if things go badly.

• When weighing the consequences of your decisions, take into account those that are long-term, as well as those that will result in the short-term.

• Prepare and anticipate the management of the possible effects of your decisions; in this way you will be able to adequately react if they present themselves.

• *Keep in mind the three aspects of effective decision-making: efficiency, impact on others and impact on oneself.*

09.

Put What You Decide On Into Practice

Close to 11:30pm, the *Titanic* continued its voyage at the considerable speed of 20.5 nautical miles per hour, despite the darkness of night and poor visibility. The temperature had fallen significantly. At that moment, one of the ship's lookouts, Frederick Fleet, saw an enormous mass of ice less than ½ a kilometer in the distance. Quickly, he gave a warning signal and called the officer on duty who was at his post. A few seconds later, there was a collision.

From the time that Fleet sighted the iceberg until the time that the crash occurred, they only had a bit more than 30 seconds to avoid the collision. Why did this situation happen? Why is it that when the lookout saw the iceberg, the ship was so close to it that it barely had time to react? The poor visibility that existed on that night and the ship's excessive speed were factors that influenced the matter so that when the iceberg was spotted, it was already much too late.

Certain experts affirm that if the iceberg had been sighted 60 seconds in advance instead of 30 seconds ahead of time, the collision could have been avoided. So, if the lookouts had had binoculars it is more than likely that the collision could have been avoided. But since Fleet did not have the adequate resources to perform his job in an efficient manner, he could not do this. Without sufficient resources, we cannot apply decisions we make. Therefore, before making a decision, it is necessary to ascertain that the minimum necessary resources are available in order to implement the decision; then, after making that decision one must facilitate those minimum resources so that the decision can be executed.

The most striking fact about the lack of binoculars on the part of the guards on duty is the fact that since the lookouts did not have binoculars, this does not mean that there weren't any on the ship. The officials all had them at their disposal, but it did not occur to any of them to lend them out to the lookouts so that they could do their job. *The resources existed, but they were not in the hands of those who needed them the most: the lookouts, but rather in the possession of those with more power: the officials.*

The captain's reaction time was not considerably long. From the time they went to wake him, he went up to the command post, then went down to the place of the collision to evaluate the damage, but these trips consumed 30 minutes of the two hours that, according to the warnings of the architect, the ship would remain afloat. He had, therefore, 90 minutes to attempt to minimize the impact of the sinking. So what is it that the captain did during that time? He made decisions: the first, to send SOS signals, and the second, to make use of the lifeboats.

After returning from the damage reconnaissance, the captain's first reaction was directed at the radio hall, giving the radio operators instructions that they constantly emit help calls so that other ships could come to their rescue. The operators did that work until shortly before sinking without obtaining satisfactory results. At the same time, he also ordered the launching of light signals so that other ships could see them. But the results were also not positive. Despite carrying out these activities for an hour and a half, they did not obtain any type of effective response and even still they continued doing this until the end. *They persevered in carrying out some efforts that were in vain considering what they achieved.*

The captain's second decision, after ordering the constant dispatch of messages asking for help and light signals, was to make use of the lifeboats. As previously mentioned, there were clearly insufficient boats onboard for all of the passengers and the crew, but the management of these also did not help save more lives.

Two factors seriously hampered the evacuation: the first was that the officials were not capable of filling the lifeboats and many of them were lowered almost empty. This can be explained, on the one hand, because they did not have the previous experience nor the specific practice to rapidly and efficient manage the *Titanic's* lifeboats, nor did they understand the true capacity of the boats. Furthermore, when the evacuation to the lifeboats was initiated, 30 minutes had already gone by since the collision, that is to say, approximately one fourth of the time left before sinking. Had this activity started to be carried out earlier, the evacuation could have been done more calmly, and the lifeboats could have gone out with more passengers.

Had they taken better advantage of time, made the decision to start to fill the lifeboats in advance, and if they had previously established systems and procedures for rescue operations, they could have saved more people than they did. Working without time greatly hampers positive results and, because of this, it is advised to plan the time that is available in order to make and implement decisions.

The second factor that complicated the efficiency of the evacuation was that many of those who were meant to occupy the lifeboats, only women and children without any belongings, did not want to do so as they did not wish to abandon their husbands or because they had a greater sensation of security onboard the *Titanic* than on a small lifeboat in the middle of the ocean on such a cold dark night. Because only women and children could occupy the lifeboats, some men attempted to board them by force and which it was necessary for the officials in charge of the evacuation to fire deterrent shots into the air on several occasions. On one of these occasions, shots were fired at three passengers causing their deaths. Some of the more important men from first class also occupied places within the lifeboats, just as Bruce Ismay, the general director of White Star, did.

When the lifeboats were lowered at around 2 am, the captain, who perished in the sinking, released all members of the crew from his responsibility, telling them that they had accomplished their duties and that they each had to take care of themselves. The 1,500 people who still remained onboard the ship waited to definitely sink without being able to do anything. At that moment, many of the passengers and members of the crew threw themselves desperately into the sea. Almost none of the lifeboats that were half empty went to rescue them. They drowned. At around 2:15am the *Titanic* broke into two parts, producing a great roar, and it sunk at a very fast speed. The catastrophe was a reality.

The consequences of not being able to fill the lifeboats were very palpable: in the case that they had been filled completely it is calculated that at least 600 more people could have been saved, that is to say, double the amount of the 700 who were actually saved. Here the question was not about not having resources, that is to say lifeboats, but also how the management of these was deficient, because they were not able to take advantage of the available capacity. The management of resources is not solely a matter of the quantity of means available, but also a question of the good or bad use of these means.

The *Carpathia* did not only change its course immediately after receiving the first call for help, but it also augmented its velocity to arrive faster. Its normal velocity was set at 14.5 nautical miles per hour, but the captain set the ship's speed at 17.5 nautical miles, even risking damage to the ship. It took the ship four hours to arrive, doing so after 4 am. Fortunately, it was possible for all of the survivors to board on the ship.

The *Carpathia* went full speed ahead in the direction of the ice against which the *Titanic* had crashed. Since it could not reduce its speed so as to not delay the rescue, it secured risk reduction for collision by adding a man to its guard post, two more on the stern, and others on each side of the command post. In this way, they were able to avoid five large icebergs that they encountered. Both captains, Smith and Rostron, made the same decision to pass through the iceberg zone, but the manner in which they did so determined the results.

The gravest part about the *California*'s reaction was that if it has reacted adequately upon seeing the *Titanic*'s light signals, she could have arrived to the location of the incident before the sinking, and would have saved all of the lives. In fact, in the investigation after the catastrophe that the English authorities carried out, the *Californian's* reaction was condemned as negligent.

But it was not until 5:30 am on the 15th of April that a ship, the *Frankfurt*, was informed about the sinking of the *Titanic*. When they arrived at the scene, they could not help anybody. On the one hand, the lifeboat survivors had already been saved by another ship, the *Carpathia*, which, as already stated, was more than five times farther than theirs had been at the moment of the accident, and by this time, the victims were already a irremediable reality.

They ended up making the same efforts, if not more, than if they had directed themselves to the *Titanic* after receiving the first light signal, but in arriving late, their efforts were useless. Arriving late, is often as efficient as not arriving at all. Similarly, *making a decision without thinking whether it is the opportune moment to implement it could lead to making efforts to realize it that do not mean much.*

* * *

Making a decision is a fundamental element but executing it, in other words, putting it into practice, is even more fundamental. In order to achieve effectiveness, the decision needs to be followed by action. We may have gone with one of the best solutions possible, but if then it is not acted on, the impact is null. Investing time in making a decision is useless if it cannot be applied. A decision that is not carried out in practice does not serve for anything and does not impact reality. No decision is good until someone does something with it. Therefore, one of the criteria at the time of decision-making is its applicability. Often decisions are made that appear adequate on paper but that later are not possible to implement.

Putting decisions into practice that solely depend on us, in principle, only depends on our will. For example, if we decide to go to the gym twice a week, under normal circumstances this is something that we need to put into practice ourselves, without depending on others. By executing our will we can put our decisions into practice.

The problem arrives when the decision has been made and we do not place sufficient determination into it and ultimately abandon it. These situations are in the habit of affecting our self-esteem. If one proposes to learn English one hour a day every day, and after a short time stops doing so because one does not feel like it, then the result is debilitating since confidence in one's willpower is lost.

But there are decisions that do not solely depend on ourselves, like, for example, if our decision is to go to the gym with a certain friend, then actually doing so is not entirely dependent on our own effort, but also in convincing our friend to go, as well. The major portion of the decisions we make, and even more so within entrepreneurial environments, are of this type; in other words, in order to be able to apply decisions we will need to convince third party members, whether they are clients, bosses, suppliers, colleagues or collaborators. Sometimes we need them to authorize a budget in order to implement our decision or for them to facilitate certain resources or that they remove other responsibilities... In this case, before making the decision, we must analyze if it will be possible to count on the support of those we will need in order to carry it out.

On one occasion, the director of a company made the resolution to install a switchboard that could divert telephone calls so that when the people at reception had to move, they could attend to the telephone at the same time. But since reception was not directly responsible to him, the manager aborted the initiative because though the proposal was efficient, he considered it meddling.

The radical question is that not only do we have to make a decision, but also treat those people affected by our decision adequately to create allies that will support it. The decisions also need to be "sold". When we make a decision, if we want it to be "accepted", we have to see who is affected by it and how, and once we identify the principle actors, make the case for the benefits that they will obtain if they decided to support our decision.

Before making a decision it is advisable to carry out an analysis in order to manage its implementation. In order to carry out this type of analysis we can ask ourselves who will need to support this in order to put it into practice, then identify how what I am proposing will affect them, and finally, elaborate on the benefits that they may obtain in the case that they do support you. If we have this information it will be easier to manage the compliance of the rest with our decision.

SUMMARY OF IDEAS

• A good decision needs to be able to be put into practice.

• A decision that is not put into practice does not serve for anything because it does not impact reality. No decision is good until someone does something with it.

• Make decisions, but then pay attention to how you will execute them, because the results depend on how they are implemented.

• Analyze whom you may need to convince in order to apply your decisions and identify their interests: "sell" your ideas to those they affect so that they can be applied.

• Take into account that it is customary for there to be differences in how you think things will go and how things actually go.

10.

Be Conscious That Not Everything Is Rational

Since management wanted ample spaces on the ship at all cost, they applied pressure on the technicians in order to achieve this space on the basis of eliminating security elements. That is to say, they did not take into account the experts' initial design and they applied pressure to change this in function of their interests. They made decisions about the construction of the ship, placing security in danger and ignoring the experts.

The fact that managers had the last word for making a decision about the construction of the ship and that they did it without sufficiently listening to the experts led them to make harmful decisions. Had they taken into account the arguments made by the engineers, the security would have been different. *But they opted to decide to prioritize their particular interests above the general interests.*

The election of the captain of the ship was a fundamental decision, seeing as how he was ultimately responsible for everything occurring on the vessel. The general director of the naval company, Bruce Ismay, who, as we mentioned, survived the sinking by occupying one of the scarce places in the lifeboats, was finally responsible for this designation.

Ismay opted for captain John Smith, a veteran of the White Star line, who stated before the *Titanic's* departure that this would be his last voyage, considering that he had made the decision to retire. Alas, he died in the sinking. Why did Ismay select Smith? The ultimate reasons are probably only known by Smith himself, but the captain was recognized in the naval world for two apparent reasons. On the one hand, he was a genuine public relations person who enjoyed great popularity in general, and especially among the wealthiest classes. If the *Titanic* were to be a floating luxury hotel, then who better to navigate it then the most "glamorous" captain? His fame could have been the reason that he charged twice what all the other captains charged. On the other hand, he was known for his preference for speed. This inclination led him to have three notable accidents over the span of ten years. Taking into account that Ismay had announced to the press that the ship would arrive at its destination one day before what had been predicted, Captain Smith, with his love of speed, was a good candidate for achieving this goal.

These characteristics, popularity and velocity, had consequences in the unraveling of the tragedy. On the one side, the devotion of the captain to public relations reasons led him to be at a dinner in his honor, organized by one of the passengers in first class, instead of being attentive to all that was happening on the control deck. This is despite that fact that he was conscious that they were traversing an iceberg zone and that visibility was poor. On the other hand, his fondness for velocity led him to not reduce the ship's speed despite the warnings that there were icebergs, and to continue navigating at a speed more than double the recommended speed in such a situation at sea at the time of collision on the night of the accident.

If, instead of a public relations figure with such fondness for velocity, Ismay had selected, for example, a prudent and cautious captain, on the night of the accident the captain would have probably been directing the operations at the control deck, and he would have considerably reduced the velocity, including stopping the engine, just as some of the other ships who found themselves in that zone did. In this way, the crash could have been avoided, or, at the very least, the collision would have been softer. Criteria such as popularity or affection for speed in a captain were not exactly the most rational arguments for making a decision about who would be guiding the ship.

From the moment the lookouts warned of the presence of icebergs, First Officer Murdoch had less than one minute to react. During this time, he ordered the steersman to turn to the left, and the engine room to stop the motors and to reverse at maximum velocity. Were these maneuverings adequate to avoid or minimize the effects of the accident?

According to the experts, the maneuverings that were realized were mistaken, taking into account the proximity to the iceberg. It is certain that with such measures a frontal collision was avoided; at the same time, this caused a lateral collision with the front part of the vessel on the right-hand side of the ship, considered the most vulnerable part of the ship. Ift the collision had been frontal, only three or four watertight compartments would have been destroyed, permitting the ship to continue to stay afloat. Meanwhile, a lateral collision caused six out of the six compartments to be ruptured which impeded the ship from maintaining itself above water.

If a frontal collision had been permitted to happen most probably the ship would not have sunk. But, as we have pointed out, the officials did not have experience in navigating a ship of such dimensions, nor had they significantly familiarized themselves with it, or practiced maneuverings to avoid collisions. Due to lack of preparation, Murdoch was not in any condition to manage the situation in which he found himself, and given the time pressure, he reacted instinctively with what he believed to be the most rational response, but with what was not, lamentably, the most adequate response. His intuitive response was not adequate.

When there is not enough preparation, it is impossible to react rapidly in an adequate way, which is what happened with Murdoch. Therefore, it is necessary to be prepared for when it is time to react rapidly so that it is done well. If the official had practiced exercises of maneuverings, or simply if someone had explained to him that it was better to collide head on than laterally, then the sinking could have possibly been avoided. The intuitive response without previous preparation is not customarily efficient.

* * *

Theoretically, deciding in a rational way is the most adequate. But, human beings are not just rational. Even when we intend to be rational, emotional impulses emerge. From a rational point of view, playing the lottery or betting in pools, is foolish. As a whole, money is always lost (in a contrary case the organizer of the lottery would lose it and nobody would end up ahead). Nevertheless, in some circumstances it may be that a good decision, the mental worth of the emotion and happiness that we may gain may be superior to the economic cost of participating in the game. When all is said and done, there is always someone who ends up winning.

Our point of departure is that we are rational, but reality tells us that we are not only rational. Human beings also have feelings. Because of this, we frequently make decisions that are not strictly based on reason. And this face is not good or bad as such, it simply is. As people, we have two dimensions—the rational and the sentimental—that operate in us at decision-making time. Therefore rationality is imperfect; it has some limits. Some of these are of a personal character, that is to say, unique to the individual, and others of an organizational character, or, belonging to the organizations in which decision-making unfolds.

In the organizational context, distinct persons and groups can have different interests from other collectives and persons, and even from those of the organization itself. The search for individual benefit or of defined groups can complicate, in certain ways, the rationality of decisions. The Hurricane Katrina disaster is a good example.

This hurricane battered the city of New Orleans, in the state of Louisiana, on the 30th of August, 2005. The American scientist, Mark Fischeti, had already published an article in *Scientific American* where he described everything that would happen to the city of New Orleans. It turns out that diverse hurricanes like Hurricane Andrew in 1992 or Hurricane Betsy in 1967, citing the most violent, happened frequently on the US coast off the Gulf of Mexico, and that scientists from various universities in Texas and from the southern US had already developed data simulations that forecasted what would happen in the city of New Orleans when a hurricane of such great intensity hit.

New Orleans is, like the Netherlands, below sea level. Dams protected it from the ocean, but they impeded the dirt that the Mississippi river dragged along with it from settling and that the river's delta develop a foothold in the city. Those same dams that protected the city are what provoked its flooding. It was only a matter of years. Sooner or later it would occur. It was a disaster waiting to happen.

Nevertheless, nothing was done to avoid the disaster. Diverse propositions for interventions to defend the city from possible hurricanes had been made. But the different local groups— the oil companies, and oyster producers, etc.— applied pressure on Washington to finance and protect their respective projects and interests, so that amid so many petitions the matter of protecting the city from a possible hurricane was left diluted amongst other projects, so that it never managed to become a priority.

We have seen similar situations to those of Hurricane Katrina in the cases of the Titanic where the interest in arriving earlier than expected led to the making of decisions that were irrational, such as not decreasing velocity and not changing the route; and, in the Enron case, where individual interests of a few managers also led to the falsification of accounting in order for them to become richer.

The search of individual interests is articulated in what has come to be called "politicking". Politicking consists of distinct parts of an organization, whether individuals or groups of individuals, seeking their own objectives. The situation is that an organization is collection of groups that are each seeking their own interests. In the end, the criteria of the strongest group prevails. The one that has more power succeeds. The consequence for the company is that organizational objectives are not sought, but rather the individual objectives of groups are sought out. This makes it very difficult for an organization to make progress.

But, this struggle to impose one's particular criteria or a group's criteria, never provides an optimal solution. The distinct parts hide relevant information from the other parts. Information does not flow, which makes it difficult to obtain the best solution for the problem. Politicking in organizations leads to the formation of coalitions to augment power and, in this way, to be able to impose alternatives that benefit one in particular. It is unusual for the best alternative for the organization come to the surface. In the end, everything ends in a struggle for power.

The fact that, in many cases, internal decisions of a company are made in groups, also makes it customary for rationality to be limited, now that, with this type of decision the people tend to support what the majority have decided as a result of the unconscious pressure exerted by the groups for which individuals adopt a decision that they think will be the most accepted. Group thinking entails pressure to reach unanimity— that way each of its members gain acceptance.

In order to avoid the possible irrationality that occurs in when making decisions in groups, it is convenient to either invite an outsider from the group to give his or her opinion, or to give one of the members of the group, the role of "devil's advocate", and make sure that this function always rotates amongst members.

As previously stated, apart from organizational themes, there are personal factors—and these are the most relevant— that limit rationality. There are types of people who are accustomed to making decisions based on feelings rather than on reason. That is to say, they utilize both elements, but they emphasize the emotional side more. These people are characterized as more interested in people than in things. They tend to be diplomatic and to express themselves with tact so as to not disturb the rest. They customarily are in agreement with those they have around them, and are naturally friendly and amiable. Because of all this, they tend to be adept in putting together social activities.

This type of person, if he or she had to let go of a collaborator, would tend to consider his or her personal and family situation before doing so. Meanwhile, the type of person who gives more weight to reason than to his or her feelings, at the hour of deciding a whether to lay someone off, would give more relevance to aspects related to productivity of the situation than to those of the collaborator's personal situation.

The type of person who emphasizes rationality more is characterized as valuing logic above all else, and is more centered on things than on people. This type of person says what he or she thinks although it could bother others. He or she tends to have more developed executive abilities than social ones, and is very apt at organizing facts and ideas in clear presentations.

Keeping in mind these two profiles, it is that one of the two is more adequate for making a decision efficiently. But the question is, in a way, irrelevant, because a person is either one way or another. What is fundamental is that each person knows his or her tendency— rational or emotional— in order to be able to manage it adequately. In other words, those who emphasize rationality more when making decisions should intend to have the sentimental factor in mind more when the time comes to make a decision; and vice versa, the one who naturally emphasizes the emotional aspects more, should be conscious of this so as to include more rational criteria in his or her decisions.

Another point is that all people more or less have a tendency to operate a series of distorted thoughts that lead them to perceive reality through a distinct lens. The forms of distorted thought that are most common are: those that a person who is faced with a situation where there are positive and negative aspects, gives special emphasis to the negative aspects, and barely pays attention to the positive ones and vice versa. Within these types of people, there are also people who have a tendency to perceive things in extremes, without allowing for a middle ground. Other common forms of distorted thoughts include:

to generalize, or taking as truth at a universal level an observation that has only been observed in one particular and concrete case; to label, in other words, from one concrete quality about a person, to make a global judgment about them, and to believe that what we consider to be "just" must be equally so for the rest. Similarly, at an individual level, personal habits that limit rationality include fear, aversion to risk, stress, insecurity, confusion, etc.

In order to make correct decisions it is fundamental to known ourselves well: what are our weak points and our strong points when it comes time to make a decision. By knowing how we think and how we decide, we avoid errors that can be avoided, and, above all else, we can go about learning from the errors committed.

In the end, deciding well consists of an adequate combination of reason and intuition. Intuition is very useful if it is accompanied by reason. Intuition is an unconscious process that operates collectively, different from the rational processes; intuition first breaks down the situation into parts, analyzes each of these and then combines them to form a whole again. Intuition is a rapid process, almost instantaneous and emotions and affects intervene in this process before reason.

Intuition is something that works at the subconscious level. We intuit that something is good but we do not know the reasons why, but we have a sensation. If we were able to say why it would no longer be intuition; it would be reason. Intuition is something complex that is managed in a subtle and inexplicable way: data and objective information together with subjective impressions. It is fast, so intuition, without reason, can be a shortcut to arriving at conclusions.

There are two types of intuition. On the one hand, we have intuition that is "suspicious" of something: we have to decide something and we suspect that this alternative is the most adequate. We do not know why but we have a strong hunch. On the other hand, we have intuition that is "automatic routine": based on having confronted a determined type of situation many times, we end up becoming experts in "this" and we recognize intuitively what we should do at each moment.

It is knowledge that a doctor has from the accumulation of past experiences, so that by only looking at the face of a sick person or asking a few questions the doctor knows what his ailment is. It is the experience that a firefighter has who knows intuitively what must be done when facing a situation of grave risk, in which it is necessary to act quickly without time to analyze the distinct alternatives. It is the experience acquired by expert chess players, who can participate in various matches simultaneously. Each time the player changes boards he or she recognizes the situation and knows what needs to be done without having to analyze all of the possible plays. Basing ourselves in experience and in acquired knowledge, we can intuitively discern what the best alternative for a given situation is.

Intuition that is automated routine is not good for finding creative solutions to problems. It is good for dealing with recognizable situations to save the effort of having to analyze them. We have them synthesized in our experience and can trust in our intuition to let us know that we are acting correctly.

Intution that is suspicious is very useful for generating alternatives. It is good for finding new possible methods to face situations and to propose creative and distinct solutions to the problems we face. But this type of suspicious intution always requires a detailed analysis to know if the decision makes sense or not. Before a distinct solution, it is impossible to know from habit with certainty if it will work or not, until we put it into practice. When all is said and done, it is something new. What criteria do we have to know if this new solution makes sense or not.

There are three conditions that these types of intuitive solutions should meet to justify whether to try them or not. Firstly, realize that this situation presupposes some controlled risk. In other words, if the worst is to happen, this does not translate into an authentic disaster, neither for us nor for the company. Secondly, the intuitive solution should only be tried once everything that can be analyzed has been tried. In other words, we cannot go about dumbly and wildly making decisions with the excuse that they are intuitive, then observe what happens next. And finally, it should generate learning, just as much if things go well or if they go badly, it is good to learn along the way to avoid possible errors in the future.

SUMMARY OF IDEAS

• We are rational beings with feelings, and the latter also intervene in decision-making.

• Rationality is imperfect and it has limitations so much in its individual character, as in organizational character.

• The most relevant organizational limits are conflict of interests of people and pressure that groups apply when making decisions.

• It is best to have equilibrium between reason and emotion, and that neither of these two prevail over the other: the person who is more sentimental needs to make an effort to be more rational and vice versa.

• Intuition accompanied by reason is very useful for making decisions.

CONCLUSION

Making decisions and putting them into practice is the most important task, not only for managers, but for individuals as well. This is the case because our lives, just as the organizations of which we are a part, are dependent upon the decisions that we make. It can be said that our biographies, and those of the companies alike, are a history of successive decisions that we have adopted...across time. External factors exist that we cannot influence, but those things that we have the capacity to influence, we influence through the decisions that we make and in their subsequent implementations. Therefore, it is important to learn to decide well.

In this book we have picked a series of fundamental principles that need to be taken into account to guaraneee that we are well-positioned for making our decisions. Following these also gives us the possibility of learning each time to make better decisions. We learn to decide when we internalize some basic principles, which are those that we have outlined in the previous chapters.

We make decisions to resolve problems. And, we think that if we have solved something that we have decided well, and if we have not resolved something that then we have decided badly. But as we have seen, although we may have been able to resolve a problem that we had, we might have made a bad decision. This is because the decisions that we make, in addition to resolving or not resolving the problem that led to making the decision, can also have another type of consequence, that when not considered, can generate a greater problem.

The fact of deciding well does not imply that one reaches the objectives that were targeted which makes it difficult to learn to decide simply on the basis of deciding. On the other hand, the major consequence of deciding well is that every time we are in a better condition to decide better, and, on the contrary, by deciding badly, perhaps we are in worse circumstances to decide the next time.

In summary, we cannot judge the quality of a decision by its results, but by the process that has been undertaken to make a better decision. Have the basic principles of correct decision-making been used? If yes, well then the desired results will have been attained and learning will be produced.

Making decisions is a necessity, an obligation and a responsibility. If we do not make them, life will continue on its course and it will be circumstances, in the best of cases, that make these decisions for us; and, in the worst of cases, it will be other people who take control of our lives. If we want to govern our lives, let us make our own decisions, and if we want to make good decisions, let us follow the principles explained in this book.